The Strong-Willed Child

BIRTH THROUGH ADOLESCENCE

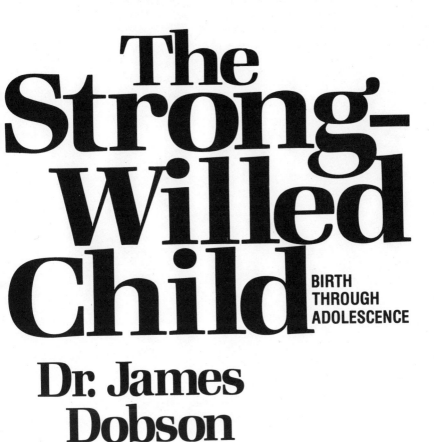

The Strong-Willed Child

BIRTH THROUGH ADOLESCENCE

Dr. James Dobson

TYNDALE
HOUSE
PUBLISHERS, INC.

Wheaton, Illinois

Library of Congress Catalog Card Number 77–083559
ISBN 0–8423–0664–1, cloth

Copyright © 1978 Tyndale House Publishers, Inc.,
Wheaton, Illinois 60187

First printing, February 1978
Printed in the United States of America

Contents

Introduction

A woman with seven rambunctious children boarded a Los Angeles bus and sat in the seat behind me. Her hair was a mess and the gaunt look on her face revealed a state of utter exhaustion. As she stumbled past me with her wiggling tribe, I asked, "Do all these children belong to you, or is this some kind of picnic!"

She looked at me through sunken eyes and said, "They're all mine, and believe me, it's *no* picnic!"

I smiled to myself, understanding fully what she meant. Small children have an uncanny ability to unravel an adult nervous system. They are noisy and they make incredible messes and they bicker with one another and their noses drip and they scratch the furniture and they have more energy in their fat little fingers than mama has in her entire weary body.

There's no doubt about it: children are expensive little people. To raise them properly will require the *very best* that you can give of your time, effort, and financial resources. However, to those who have never experienced parenthood, the job may appear ridiculously simple. Such people remind me of a man watching the game of golf for the first time, thinking, "That looks easy. All you have to do is hit that little white ball out there in the direction of the flag." He then steps up to the tee, draws back his club, and dribbles the "little white ball" about nine feet to the left. Accordingly, I should warn those who have not yet assumed the responsibilities of parenthood: the game of raising kids is more difficult than it looks.

So parenthood is costly and complex. Am I suggesting, then, that newly married couples should remain childless? Certainly not! The family that loves children and wants to experience the thrill of procreation should not be frightened by the challenge of parenthood. Speaking from my own perspective as a father, there has been no greater moment in my life than when I gazed into the eyes of my infant daughter, and five years later, my son. What could be more exciting than seeing those tiny human beings begin to blossom and grow and learn and love? And what reward could be more meaningful than having my little boy or girl climb onto my lap as I sit by the fire, hug my neck and whisper, "I love you, Dad." Oh, yes, children are expensive, but they're worth the price. Besides, nothing worth having comes cheap.

Furthermore, many of the frustrations of parenthood occur because we have no well-designed model or "game plan" to follow in response to the inevitable circumstances that develop. Then when the routine, predictable problems occur, we try to muddle through by random trial and error. Such parents remind me of a friend who flew his single-engine airplane toward a small country airport. He arrived as the sun had dropped behind a mountain at the close of the day, and by the time he maneuvered his plane into position to land, he could not see the hazy field below. He had no lights on his plane and there was no one on duty at the airport. He circled the runway for another attempt to land, but the darkness had then become even more impenetrable. For two hours he flew his plane around and around in the blackness of night, knowing that he faced certain death when his fuel was expended. Then as greater panic gripped him, a miracle occurred. Someone on the ground heard the continuing drone of his engine and realized his predicament. That merciful man drove his car back and forth on the runway to show my friend the location of the airstrip, and then let his lights cast their beam from the far end while the plane landed.

I think of that story whenever I am descending at night in a commercial airliner. As I look ahead, I can see the green lights bordering the runway which tell the captain where to direct the plane. If he stays between those lighted boundaries, all will be well. There is safety in that illuminated zone, but disaster lies to the left or right.

Isn't that what we need as parents? There should be clearly marked boundaries that tell us where to steer the family ship. We require some guiding *principles* which will help us raise our children in safety and health. It should be apparent by now that my purpose in this book is to provide some of those understandings which will contribute to competent parenthood. We will deal particularly with the subject of discipline as it relates to the "strong-willed child." Most parents have at least one such youngster who seems to be born with a clear idea of how he wants the world to be operated and an intolerance for those who disagree. Even in infancy, he fairly bristles when his dinner is late and he insists that someone hold him during every waking hour. Later, during toddlerhood he declares total war on all forms of authority, at home or abroad, and his greatest thrill comes from drawing on the walls and flushing kitties down the toilet. His parents are often guilt-ridden and frustrated people who wonder where they've gone wrong and why their home life is so different than they were led to expect.

We'll be investigating this self-propelled youngster during his progression through childhood, including infancy, toddlerhood, early and late elementary school years, and (brace yourself) during adolescence. Our discussion will also consider his behavior as it relates to sibling rivalry, hyperactivity, and the foundations of self-esteem.

It is my firm conviction that the strong-willed child usually possesses more creative potential and strength of character than his compliant siblings, provided his parents can help him channel his impulses and gain control of his rampaging will. My writings are dedicated to this purpose.

In short, this book is designed to provide *practical* advice and suggestions to parents who may be reacting to these more difficult challenges without design or forethought. And if I've been successful, this discourse may offer a lighted runway to pilots who circle in the darkness above.

James Dobson, Ph.D.

1 The Wild and Woolly Will

The Dobson household consists of a mother and father, a boy and a girl, one hamster, a parakeet, one lonely gold-fish, and two hopelessly neurotic cats. We all live together in relative harmony with a minimum of conflict and strife. But there is another member of our "family" who is less congenial and cooperative. He is a stubborn twelve-pound dachshund named Sigmund Freud (Siggie), who honestly believes he owns the place. All dachshunds tend to be somewhat independent, I'm told, but Siggie is a confirmed revolutionary. He's not vicious or mean; he just wants to run things—and the two of us have been engaged in a power struggle for the past twelve years.

Siggie is not only stubborn, but he doesn't pull his own weight in the family. He won't bring in the newspaper on cold mornings; he refuses to "chase a ball" for the children; he doesn't keep the gophers out of the garden; and he can't do any of the usual tricks that most cultured dogs perform. Alas, Siggie has refused to participate in any of the self-improvement programs I have initiated on his behalf. He is content just to trot through life, watering and sniffing and stopping to smell the roses.

Furthermore, Sigmund is not even a good watchdog. This suspicion was confirmed the night we were visited by a prowler who had entered our backyard at three o'clock in the morning. I suddenly awoke from a deep sleep, got out of bed, and felt my way through the house without turning on the lights. I knew someone was on the patio and Siggie knew it too, because the coward was crouched behind me! After listening to the thumping of my heart for a few minutes, I reached out to take hold of the rear doorknob. At that moment, the backyard gate quietly opened and closed. Someone had been standing three feet from me, and that "someone" was now tinkering in my garage. Siggie and I held a little conversation in the darkness and decided that he should be the one to investigate the disturbance. I opened the back door and told my dog to "attack!" But Siggie just *had* one! He stood there throbbing and shaking so badly that I couldn't even push him out the back door. In the noise and confusion that ensued, the intruder escaped, (which pleased both dog *and* man).

Please don't misunderstand me; Siggie is a member of our family and we love him dearly. And despite his anarchistic nature, I have finally taught him to obey a few simple commands. However, we had some classic battles before he reluctantly yielded to my authority. The greatest confrontation occurred a few years ago when I had been in Miami for a three-day conference. I returned to observe that Siggie had become boss of the house while I was gone. But I didn't realize until later that evening just how strongly he felt about his new position as Captain.

At eleven o'clock that night, I told Siggie to go get into his bed, which is a permanent enclosure in the family room. For six years I had given him that order at the end of each day, and for six years Siggie had obeyed. On that occasion, however, he refused to budge. You see, he was in the bathroom, seated comfortably on the furry lid of the toilet seat. That is his favorite spot in the house, because it allows him to bask in the warmth of a nearby electric heater. Incidentally, Siggie had to learn the hard way that it is extremely important that the lid be *down* before he leaves the ground. I'll never forget the night he learned that lesson. He came thundering in from the cold, sailed through the air —and nearly drowned before I could get him out.

When I told Sigmund to leave his warm seat and go to bed, he flattened his ears and slowly turned his head toward me. He deliberately braced himself by placing one paw on the edge of the furry lid, then hunched his shoulders, raised his lips to reveal the molars on both sides, and uttered his most threatening growl. That was Siggie's way of saying, "Get lost!"

I had seen this defiant mood before, and knew there was only one way to deal with it. The *only* way to make Siggie obey is to threaten him with destruction. Nothing else works. I turned and went to my closet and got a small belt to help me "reason" with Mr. Freud. My wife, who was watching this drama unfold, tells me that as soon as I left the room, Siggie jumped from his perch and looked down the hall to see where I had gone. Then he got behind her and growled.

When I returned, I held up the belt and again told my

angry dog to go get into his bed. He stood his ground so I gave him a firm swat across the rear end, and he tried to bite the belt. I hit him again and he tried to bite *me*. What developed next is impossible to describe. That tiny dog and I had the most vicious fight ever staged between man and beast. I fought him up one wall and down the other, with both of us scratching and clawing and growling and swinging the belt. I am embarrassed by the memory of the entire scene. Inch by inch I moved him toward the family room and his bed. As a final desperate maneuver, Siggie jumped up on the couch and backed into the corner for one last snarling stand. I eventually got him to bed, but only because I outweighed him 200 to 12!

The following night I expected another siege of combat at Siggie's bedtime. To my surprise, however, he accepted my command without debate or complaint, and simply trotted toward the family room in perfect submission. In fact, that fight occurred more than four years ago, and from that time to this, Siggie has never made another "go for broke" stand.

It is clear to me now that Siggie was saying in his canine way, "I don't think you're tough enough to make me obey." Perhaps I seem to be humanizing the behavior of a dog, but I think not. Veterinarians will confirm that some breeds of dogs, notably dachshunds and shepherds, will not accept the leadership of their masters until human authority has stood the test of fire and proved itself worthy.

But this is not a book about the discipline of dogs; there is an important moral to my story which is highly relevant to the world of children. *Just as surely as a dog will occasionally challenge the authority of his leaders, a little child is inclined to do the same thing, only more so.* This is no minor observation, for it represents a characteristic of human nature which is rarely recognized (or admitted) by the "experts" who write books on the subject of discipline. I have yet to find a text for parents or teachers which acknowledges the struggle—the exhausting confrontation of wills—which most parents and teachers experience regularly with their children. Adult leadership is rarely accepted unchallenged by the next generation; it must be "tested" and found worthy of allegiance by the youngsters who are asked to yield and submit to its direction.

The Hierarchy of Strength and Courage

But why are children so pugnacious? Everyone knows that they are lovers of justice and law and order and secure boundaries. The writer of the book of Hebrews in the Bible even said that an undisciplined child feels like an illegitimate son or daughter, not even belonging to his family. Why, then, can't parents resolve all conflicts by the use of quiet discussions and explanations and gentle pats on the head? The answer is found in this curious value system of children which respects strength and courage (when combined with love). What better explanation can be given for the popularity of the mythical Superman and Captain Marvel and Wonder Woman in the folk lore of children? Why else do children proclaim, "My dad can beat up your dad!"? (One child replied to that statement, "That's nothing, my *mom* can beat up my dad, too!")

You see, boys and girls care about the issue of "who's toughest." Whenever a youngster moves into a new neighborhood or a new school district, he usually has to fight (either verbally or physically) to establish himself in the hierarchy of strength. Anyone who understands children knows that there is a "top dog" in every group, and there is a poor little defeated pup at the bottom of the heap. And every child between those extremes knows where he stands in relation to the others.

Recently my wife and I had an opportunity to observe this social hierarchy in action. We invited the fourteen girls in our daughter's fifth-grade class to our home for a slumber party. It was a noble gesture, but I can tell you with sincerity that we will never do that again. It was an exhausting and sleepless night of giggling and wiggling and jumping and bumping. But it was also a very interesting evening, from a social point of view. The girls began arriving at five o'clock on Friday night, and their parents returned to pick them up at 11 o'clock Saturday morning. I met most of them for the first time that weekend, yet during those seventeen hours together, I was able to identify every child's position in the hierarchy of respect and strength. There was one queen bee who was boss of the crowd. Everyone wanted to do what she suggested, and her jokes brought raucous laughter. Then a few degrees below her was the number two princess, followed by three, four, and five. At the bottom of the list was a harassed little girl who was alienated and rejected by the entire herd. Her jokes were as clever (I thought) as those of the leader, yet no one laughed when she clowned. Her suggestions of a game or event were immediately condemned as stupid and foolish. I found myself defending this isolated girl because of the injustice of her situation. Unfortunately, there is a similar outcast or loser in every group of three or more kids (of either sex). Such is the nature of childhood.

This respect for strength and courage also makes children want to know how "tough" their leaders are. They will occasionally disobey parental instructions for the precise purpose of testing the determination of those in charge. Thus, whether you are a parent or grandparent or Boy Scout leader or bus driver or Brownie leader or a schoolteacher

I can guarantee that sooner or later, one of the children under your authority will clench his little fist and challenge your leadership. Like Siggie at bedtime, he will convey this message by his disobedient manner: "I don't think you are tough enough to make me do what you say."

This defiant game, called Challenge the Chief, can be played with surprising skill by very young children. Only yesterday a father told me of taking his three-year-old daughter to a basketball game. The child was, of course, interested in everything in the gym except the athletic contest. The father permitted her to roam free and climb on the bleachers, but he set up definite limits regarding how far she could stray. He took her by the hand and walked with her to a stripe painted on the gym floor. "You can play all around the building, Janie, but don't go past this line," he instructed her. He had no sooner returned to his seat than the toddler scurried in the direction of the forbidden territory. She stopped at the border for a moment, then flashed a grin over her shoulder to her father, and deliberately placed one foot over the line as if to say, "Whacha gonna do about it?" Virtually every parent the world over has been asked the same question at one time or another.

The entire human race is afflicted with the same tendency toward willful defiance that this three-year-old exhibited. Her behavior in the gym is not so different from the folly of Adam and Eve in the Garden of Eden. God had told them they could eat *anything* in the Garden except the forbidden fruit ("do not go past this line"). Yet they challenged the authority of the Almighty by deliberately disobeying His commandment. Perhaps this tendency toward self-will is the essence of "original sin" which has infiltrated the human family. It certainly explains why I place such stress on the proper response to willful defiance during childhood, for that rebellion can plant the seeds of personal disaster. The thorny weed which it produces may grow into a tangled briar patch during the troubled days of adolescence.

When a parent refuses to accept his child's defiant challenge, something changes in their relationship. The youngster begins to look at his mother and father with disrespect; they are unworthy of his allegiance. More important, he wonders why they would let him do such harmful things if they really loved him. The ultimate paradox of childhood is that boys and girls want to be led by their parents, but insist that their mothers and fathers earn the right to lead them.

It is incredible to me that this aspect of human nature is so poorly recognized in our permissive society. Let me repeat my observation that the most popular textbooks for parents and teachers fail even to acknowledge that parenthood involves a struggle or contest of wills. Books and articles written on the subject of discipline usually relate not to willful defiance but to *childish irresponsibility*. There is an enormous difference between the two categories of behavior.

A 1975 article in *Family Circle* magazine[1] is typical of the watery stuff fed to parents. The title proclaimed "A Marvelous New Way to Make Your Child Behave," which should have been the first clue as to the nature of its content. (If its recommendations were so fantastic, why weren't the insights observed in more than 5000 years of parenting?) The subtitle was even more revealing, however, and it stated, "Rewards and Punishment Don't Work." Those two pollyanna-ish headlines revealed the primrose path down which the authors were leading us. Never once did they admit that a child is capable of spitting in his parent's face, or running down the middle of a busy street, or sawing a leg off the dining room table, or trying to flush baby brother down the toilet. There was no acknowledgement that some mothers and fathers go to bed at night with a pounding, throbbing headache, wondering how parenthood became such an exhausting and nerve-wracking experience. Instead, the examples given in the article focused on relatively minor incidents of childish irresponsibility: how to get your child to wash his hands before dinner, or wear the proper clothing, or take out the garbage. Responsible behavior is a noble objective for our children, but let's admit that the heavier task is shaping the child's *will!*

Strength of the Will

I have been watching infants and toddlers during recent years, and have become absolutely convinced that at the moment of birth there exists in children an inborn temperament which will play a role throughout life.

Though I would have denied the fact fifteen years ago, I am now certain that the personalities of newborns vary tremendously, even before parental influence is exercised. Every mother of two or more children will affirm that each of her infants had a different personality—a different "feel" —from the first time they were held. Numerous authorities in the field of child development now agree that these complex little creatures called babies are far from "blank slates" when they enter the world. One important study[2] by Chess, Thomas, and Birch revealed nine kinds of behaviors in which babies differ from one another. These differences tend to persist into later life and include level of activity, responsiveness, distractibility, and moodiness, among others.

Another newborn characteristic (not mentioned by

Chess) is most interesting to me and relates to a feature which can be called "strength of the will." Some children seem to be born with an easygoing, compliant attitude toward external authority. As infants they don't cry very often and they sleep through the night from the second week and they goo at the grandparents and they smile while being diapered and they're very patient when dinner is overdue. And, of course, they never spit up on the way to church. During later childhood, they love to keep their rooms clean and they especially like to do their homework and they can entertain themselves for hours. There aren't many of these supercompliant children, I'm afraid, but they are known to exist in some households, (not my own).

Just as surely as some children are naturally compliant, there are others who seem to be defiant upon exit from the womb. They come into the world smoking a cigar and yelling about the temperature in the delivery room and the incompetence of the nursing staff and the way things are run by the administrator of the hospital. They expect meals to be served the instant they are ordered, and they demand every moment of mother's time. As the months unfold, their expression of willfulness becomes even more apparent, the winds reaching hurricane force during toddlerhood.

In thinking about these compliant and defiant characteristics of children, I sought an illustration which would explain the vastly differing thrust of human temperaments. I found an appropriate analogy in a supermarket shortly thereafter. Imagine yourself in a grocery store, pushing a wire cart up the aisle. You give the basket a small shove and it glides at least nine feet out in front, and then comes to a gradual stop. You walk along happily tossing in the soup and ketchup bottles and loaves of bread. Marketing is such an easy task, for even when the cart is burdened with goods, it can be directed with one finger.

But buying groceries is not always so blissful. On other

occasions, you select a shopping cart which ominously awaits your arrival at the front of the market. When you push the stupid thing forward, it tears off to the left and knocks over a stack of bottles. Refusing to be outmuscled by an empty cart, you throw all of your weight behind the handle, fighting desperately to keep the ship on course. It seems to have a mind of its own as it darts toward the eggs and careens back in the direction of the milk and almost crushes a terrified grandmother in green tennis shoes. You are trying to do the same shopping assignment that you accomplished with ease the day before, but the job feels more like combat duty today. You are exhausted by the time you herd the contumacious cart toward the check stand.

What is the difference between the two shopping baskets? Obviously, one has straight, well-oiled wheels which go where they are guided. The other has crooked, bent wheels that refuse to yield. Do you recognize how this illustration relates to children? We might as well face it, some kids have "crooked wheels"! They do not want to go where they are led, for their own inclinations would take them in other directions. Furthermore, the mother who is "pushing the cart" must expend seven times the energy to make it move, compared with the parent of a child with "straight, well-oiled wheels." (Only mothers of strong-willed children will *fully* comprehend the meaning of this illustration.)

But how does the "typical" or "average" child respond? My original assumption was that children in the Western world probably represented a "normal" or bell-shaped curve with regard to strength of the will. In other words, I presumed there were a few very compliant kids and an equally small number who were defiant, but the great majority of youngsters were likely to fall somewhere near the middle of the distribution. (See Fig. 1.)

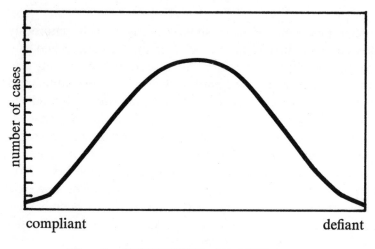

Fig. 1   STRENGTH OF THE WILL

However, having talked to at least 25,000 harried parents, I'm convinced that my supposition was wrong. The true distribution probably is depicted in Figure 2, below:

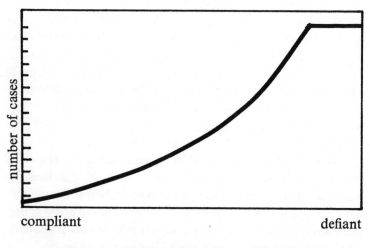

Fig. 2   STRENGTH OF THE WILL

Don't take this observation too literally, for perhaps it only *seems* that the majority of toddlers are trying to conquer the world. Furthermore, there is another phenomenon which I have never been able to explain, relating to sibling relationships. When there are two children in the family, it is likely that one youngster will be compliant and the other defiant. The easygoing child is often a genuine charmer. He smiles at least sixteen hours a day and spends most of his time trying to figure out what his parents want and how he can make them happy. In reality, he *needs* their praise and approval; thus his personality is greatly influenced by this desire to gain their affection and recognition.

The second child is approaching life from the opposite vantage point. He is sliding all four brakes and trying to gain control of the family steering mechanism. And don't you see how these differences in temperament lay the foundation for serious sibling rivalry and resentment? The defiant child faces constant discipline and hears many threats and finger-wagging lectures, while his angelic brother, little Goody-Two-Shoes, polishes his halo and soaks up the warmth of parental approval. They are pitted against each other by the nature of their divergent personalities, and may spend a lifetime scratching and clawing one another. (Chapter 4 offers specific suggestions regarding the problem of sibling rivalry and conflict.)

There are several other observations about the strong-willed child which may be helpful to his parents. First, it is reassuring to verbalize the guilt and anxiety which conscientious mothers and fathers commonly feel. They are engaged in an all-out tug of war which leaves them frustrated and fatigued. No one told them that parenthood would be this difficult, and they blame themselves for the tension that arises. They had planned to be such loving and effective parents, reading fairy stories to their pajama-clad angels by the fireplace. The difference between life as it is and life as it ought to be is a frightening and distressing bit of reality.

Furthermore, I have found that the parents of compliant children don't understand their friends with defiant youngsters. They intensify guilt and anxiety by implying, "If you would raise your kids the way I do it, you wouldn't be having those awful problems." May I say to both groups that the willful child can be difficult to control even when his parents handle him with great skill and dedication. It may take several years to bring him to a point of relative obedience and cooperation within the family unit. While this training program is in progress, it is important not to panic. Don't try to complete the transformation overnight. Treat your child with sincere love and dignity, but require him to follow your leadership. Choose carefully the matters which are worthy of confrontation, then accept his challenge on those issues and *win* decisively. Reward every positive, cooperative gesture he makes by offering your attention, affection, and verbal praise. Then take two aspirin and call me in the morning.

But the most urgent advice I can give the parents of an assertive, independent child concerns the importance of beginning to shape his will during the *early* years. I honestly believe, though the assumption is difficult to prove, that the defiant youngster is in a "high risk" category for antisocial behavior later in life. He is more likely to challenge his teachers in school and question the values he has been taught and shake his fist in the faces of those who would lead him. I believe he is more inclined toward sexual promiscuity and drug abuse and academic difficulties. This is not an inevitable prediction, of course, because the complexities of the human personality make it impossible to forecast behavior with complete accuracy. I must also stress that the overall picture is not negative. It would appear that the strong-willed child may possess more character and have greater potential for a productive life than his compliant counterpart. However, the realization of that potential may depend on a firm but loving early home environment. Thus, I repeat my admonition: begin shaping the will of that child while he is in toddlerhood. (Notice that I did not say *crush* the will, or destroy it, or snuff it out. The "how to" of that recommendation will provide the subject matter of subsequent chapters.)

QUESTIONS

Question: I'm still not sure if I understand the difference between willful defiance and childish irresponsibility. Could you explain it further?

Answer: Willful defiance, as the name implies, is a *deliberate* act of disobedience. It occurs *only* when the child knows what his parents expect and then chooses to do the opposite in a haughty manner. In short, it is a refusal to accept parental leadership, such as running away when called, screaming insults, acts of outright disobedience, etc. By contrast, childish irresponsibility results from forgetting, accidents, mistakes, a short attention span, a low frustration tolerance, immaturity, etc. In the first instance, the child knows he was wrong and is waiting to see what his parent can do about it; in the second, he has simply blundered into a consequence he did not plan. It is wrong, in my view, to resort to corporal punishment for the purpose of instilling responsibility (unless, of course, the child has defiantly refused to accept it).

Ultimately, the appropriate disciplinary reaction by a

mother or father should be determined entirely by the matter of *intention*. Suppose my three-year-old son is standing in the doorway and I say, "Ryan, please shut the door." But in his linguistic immaturity he misunderstands my statement and *opens* the door even further. Will I punish him for disobeying me? Of course not, even though he did the opposite of what I asked. He may never even know that he failed the assignment. My tolerance is dictated by his intention. He honestly tried to obey me. However, when I ask Ryan to pick up his toys, but he stamps his little foot and screams "NO!" before throwing a Tonka truck in my direction—then I am obligated to accept his challenge. In short, my child is never so likely to be punished as when I'm sure *he knows* he deserves it. And our Creator has warned of the consequences of this rebellion, stating in Proverbs 29:1, "He that being often reproved hardeneth his neck, shall suddenly be destroyed, and that without remedy" (KJV). Thus, we should teach our children to submit to our loving leadership as preparation for their later life of obedience to God.

Question: Should my child be permitted to say, "I hate you!" when he is angry?

Answer: Not in my opinion. Other writers will tell you that all children hate their parents occasionally and should be permitted to ventilate that hostility. I believe it is possible (and far more healthy) to encourage the expression of negative feelings without reinforcing temper tantrums and violent behavior. If my child screamed his hatred at me *for the first time* in a moment of red-faced anger, I would probably wait until his passion had cooled and then convey this message in a loving, sincere manner: "Charlie, I know you were very upset earlier today when we had our disagreement, and I think we should talk about what you were feeling. *All* children get angry at their parents now and then, especially when they feel unfairly treated. I understand your frustration and I'm sorry we got into such a hassle. But that does not excuse you for saying, "I hate you!" You'll learn that no matter how upset I become over something you've done, I'll *never* tell you that I hate you. And I can't permit you to talk that way to me. When people love each other, as you and I do, they don't want to hurt one another. It hurt me for you to say that you hated me, just as you would be hurt if I said something like that to you. You can, however, tell me what angers you, and I will listen carefully. If I am wrong, I will do my best to change the things you dislike. So I want you to understand that you are free to say *anything* you wish to me as always, even if your feelings are not very pleasant. But you will never be permitted to scream and call names and throw temper tantrums. If you behave in those childish ways, I will have to punish you as I would a little child. Is there anything you need to say to me now? (If not, then put your arms around my neck because I love you!)."

My purpose would be to permit the ventilation of negative feelings without encouraging violent, disrespectful, manipulative behavior.

Question: Would you, then, go so far as to apologize to a child if you felt you had been in the wrong?

Answer: I certainly would—and indeed, I have. Approximately one year ago I was burdened with pressing responsibilities which made me fatigued and irritable. One particular evening I was especially grouchy and short-tempered with my ten-year-old daughter. I knew I was not being fair, but was simply too tired to correct my manner. Through the course of the evening, I blamed Danae for things that were not her fault and upset her needlessly several times. After going to bed, I felt bad about the way I had behaved and I decided to apologize the next morning.

After a good night of sleep and a tasty breakfast, I felt much more optimistic about life. I approached my daughter before she left for school and said, "Danae, I'm sure you know that daddies are not perfect human beings. We get tired and irritable just like other people, and there are times when we are not proud of the way we behave. I know that I wasn't fair with you last night. I was terribly grouchy, and I want you to forgive me."

Danae put her arms around me and shocked me down to my toes. She said, "I knew you were going to have to apologize, Daddy, and it's okay; I forgive you."

Can there be any doubt that children are often more aware of the struggles between generations than are their busy, harassed parents?

2 Shaping the Will

The young mother of a defiant three-year-old girl approached me in Kansas City recently, to thank me for my books and tapes. She told me that a few months earlier her little daughter had become increasingly defiant and had managed to "buffalo" her frustrated mom and dad. They knew they were being manipulated but couldn't seem to regain control. Then one day they happened to see a copy of my first book, *Dare to Discipline,* on sale in a local bookstore. They bought the book and learned therein that it is appropriate to spank a child under certain well-defined circumstances. My recommendations made sense to these harassed parents, who promptly spanked their sassy daughter the next time she gave them reason to do so. But the little girl was just bright enough to figure out where they had picked up that new idea. When the mother awoke the next morning, she found her copy of *Dare to Discipline* floating in the toilet! That darling little girl had done her best to send my writings to the sewer, where they belonged. I suppose that is the strongest editorial comment I've received on any of my literature!

This incident with the toddler was not an isolated case. Another child selected my book from an entire shelf of possibilities and threw it in the fireplace. I could easily become paranoid about these hostilities. Dr. Benjamin Spock is loved by millions of children who have grown up under his influence, but I am apparently resented by an entire generation of kids who would like to catch me in a blind alley on some cloudy night.

It is obvious that children are aware of the contest of wills between generations, and that is precisely why the parental response is so important. When a child behaves in ways that are disrespectful or harmful to himself or others, his hidden purpose is often to verify the stability of the boundaries. This testing has much the same function as a policeman who turns doorknobs at places of business after dark. Though he tries to open doors, he hopes they are locked and secure. Likewise, a child who assaults the loving authority of his parents is greatly reassured when their leadership holds firm and confident. He finds his greatest security in a structured environment where the rights of other people (and his own) are protected by definite boundaries.

Our objective, then, is to *shape the will* during the early years of childhood. But how is that to be accomplished? I have talked to hundreds of parents who recognize the validity of the principle but have no idea how it can be implemented in their homes. Consequently, the remainder of this chapter has been devoted to specific suggestions and recommendations. We will begin with six broad guidelines which are paraphrased from my previous writings, followed by practical examples at each age level.

First: Define the Boundaries Before They Are Enforced

The most important step in any disciplinary procedure is to establish reasonable expectations and boundaries *in advance*. The child should know what is and what is not acceptable behavior *before* he is held responsible for those rules. This precondition will eliminate the overwhelming sense of injustice that a youngster feels when he is slapped or punished for his accidents, mistakes, and blunders. If you haven't defined it—don't enforce it!

Second: When Defiantly Challenged, Respond with Confident Decisiveness

Once a child understands what is expected, he should then be held accountable for behaving accordingly. That sounds easy, but as we have seen, most children will assault the authority of their elders and challenge their right to lead. In a moment of rebellion, a little child will consider his parents' wishes and defiantly choose to disobey. Like a military general before a battle, he will calculate the potential risks, marshal his forces and attack the enemy with guns blazing. When that nose-to-nose confrontation occurs between generations, it is *extremely* important for the adult to win decisively and confidently. The child has made it clear that he's looking for a fight, and his parents would be wise not to disappoint him! *Nothing* is more destructive to parental leadership than for a mother or father to disintegrate during that struggle. When the parent consistently loses those battles, resorting to tears and screaming and other evidence of frustration, some dramatic changes take place in the way they are "seen" by their children. Instead of being secure and confident leaders, they become spineless jellyfish who are unworthy of respect or allegiance.

Third: Distinguish between Willful Defiance and Childish Irresponsibility

A child should not be spanked for behavior that is not willfully defiant. When he forgets to feed the dog or make his bed or take out the trash—when he leaves your tennis racket outside in the rain or loses his bicycle—remember that these behaviors are typical of childhood. It is, more than likely, the mechanism by which an immature mind is protected from adult anxieties and pressures. Be gentle as you teach him to do better. If he fails to respond to your patient instruction, it then becomes appropriate to administer some well-defined consequences (he may have to work to pay for the item he abused or be deprived of its use, etc.). However, childish irresponsibility is very different from willful defiance, and should be handled more patiently.

Fourth: Reassure and Teach After the Confrontation Is Over

After a time of conflict during which the parent has demonstrated his right to lead, (particularly if it resulted in tears for the child), the youngster between two and seven (or older) may want to be loved and reassured. By all means, open your arms and let him come! Hold him close and tell him of your love. Rock him gently and let him know, again, why he was punished and how he can avoid the trouble next time. This moment of communication builds love, fidelity, and family unity. And for the Christian family, it is extremely important to pray with the child at that time, admitting to God that we have *all* sinned and no one is perfect. Divine forgiveness is a marvelous experience, even for a very young child.

Fifth: Avoid Impossible Demands

Be absolutely sure that your child is *capable* of delivering what you require. Never punish him for wetting the bed involuntarily or for not becoming potty-trained by one year of age, or for doing poorly in school when he is incapable of academic success. These impossible demands put the child in an unresolvable conflict: there is no way out. That condition brings inevitable damage to human emotional apparatus.

Sixth: Let Love Be Your Guide!

A relationship that is characterized by genuine love and affection is likely to be a healthy one, even though some parental mistakes and errors are inevitable.

To Spank or Not to Spank

With those six guidelines providing our background, let's turn our attention now to the more specific tools and techniques for shaping the will. We'll begin by discussing the practice of spanking, which has been the subject of heated controversy in recent years. More foolishness has been written on this subject than all other aspects of child rearing combined. Consider the views of Dr. John Valusek, a psychologist with whom I appeared on the Phil Donahue television show:

> The way to stop violence in America is to stop spanking children, argues psychologist John Valusek. In a speech to the Utah Association for Mental Health some weeks ago, Valusek declared that parental spanking promotes the thesis that violence against others is acceptable.
>
> "Spanking is the first half-inch on the yardstick of violence," said Valusek. "It is followed by hitting and ultimately by rape, murder, and assassination. The modeling behavior that occurs at home sets the stage: 'I will resort to violence when I don't know what else to do.' "[1]

To Dr. Valusek and his permissive colleagues I can only say, "Poppycock!" How ridiculous to blame America's obsession with violence on the disciplinary efforts of loving parents! This conclusion is especially foolish in view of the bloody fare offered to our children on television each day. The average sixteen-year-old has watched 18,000 murders during his formative years, including a daily bombardment of knifings, shootings, hangings, decapitations, and general dismemberment. Thus, it does seem strange that the psychological wizards of our day search elsewhere for the cause of brutality—and eventually point the finger of blame at the parents who are diligently training our future responsible citizens. Yet this is the kind of "press" that has been given in recent years to parents who believe in spanking their disobedient children.

Opposition to corporal punishment can be summarized by four common arguments, all of them based on error and misunderstanding. The first is represented by Dr. Valusek's statement, and assumes that spankings teach children to hit and hurt others. It depicts corporal punishment as a hostile physical attack by an angry parent whose purpose is to damage or inflict harm on his little victim. Admittedly, that kind of violence does occur regularly between generations and is tremendously destructive to children. (It is called child abuse and is discussed in the following chapter.) However, corporal punishment in the hands of a loving parent is altogether different in purpose and practice. It is a teaching tool by which harmful behavior is inhibited, rather than a wrathful attempt by one person to damage another. One is an act of love; the other is an act of hostility, and they are as different as night and day.

I responded to Dr. Valusek's argument in *Hide or Seek,* showing the place of minor pain in teaching children to behave responsibly:

"Those same specialists also say that a spanking teaches your child to hit others, making him a more violent person. Nonsense! If your child has ever bumped his arm against a hot stove, you can bet he'll never deliberately do that again. He does not become a more violent person because the stove burnt him. In fact, he learned a valuable lesson from the pain. Similarly, when he falls out of his high chair or smashes his finger in the door or is bitten by a grumpy dog, he learns about the physical dangers in his world. These bumps and bruises throughout childhood are nature's way of teaching him what to treat with respect. They do not damage his self-esteem. They do not make him vicious. They merely acquaint him with reality. In like manner, an appropriate spanking from a loving parent provides the same service. It tells him there are not only physical dangers to be avoided, but he must steer clear of some social traps as well (selfishness, defiance, dishonesty, unprovoked aggression, etc.)."[2]

The second rationale against corporal punishment can also be found in Dr. Valusek's concluding sentence, "I will resort to violence (spankings) when I don't know what else to do." Do you see the subtlety of this quotation? It characterizes a spanking as an absolute last resort—as the final act of exasperation and frustration. As such, it comes on the heels of screaming, threatening, hand-wringing, and buckets of tears. Even those authorities who recommend corporal punishment often fall into this trap, suggesting that it be applied only when all else has failed. I couldn't disagree more strongly.

A spanking is to be reserved for use in response to willful defiance, *whenever it occurs.* Period! It is much more effective to apply it early in the conflict, while the parent's emotional apparatus is still under control, than after ninety minutes of scratching and clawing. In fact, child abuse is more likely to occur when a little youngster is permitted to irritate and agitate and sass and disobey and pout for hours, until finally the parent's anger reaches a point of explosion where anything can happen (and often does). Professionals like Dr. Valusek have inadvertently contributed to violence against children, in my view, because they have stripped parents of the right to correct children's routine behavior problems while they are of minor irritation. Then when these small frustrations accumulate, the parent does (as Valusek said) "resort to violence when he doesn't know what else to do."

The third common argument against spanking comes from the findings of animal psychology. If a mouse is running in a maze, he will learn much faster if the experimentor rewards his correct turns with food than he will if his incorrect choices are punished with a mild electric shock. From this and similar studies has come the incredible assumption that punishment has little influence on human behavior. But human beings are not mice, and it is naive to equate them simplistically. Obviously, a child is capable of rebellious and defiant attitudes which have no relevance to a puzzled mouse sitting at a crossroads in a maze. I agree that it would not help a boy or girl learn to read by shocking them for each mispronounced word. On the other hand, deliberate disobedience involves the child's perception of parental authority and his obligations to accept it (whereas the mouse does not even know the experimentor exists).

If punishment doesn't influence human behavior, then why is the issuance of speeding citations by police so effective in controlling traffic on a busy street? Why, then, do homeowners rush to get their tax payments in the mail to avoid a 6 percent penalty for being late? If punishment has no power, then why does a well-deserved spanking often turn a sullen little troublemaker into a sweet and loving angel? Rat psychology notwithstanding, both reward and punishment play an important role in shaping human behavior, and neither should be discounted. Leonardo da Vinci hadn't heard about the mouse in the maze when he wrote, "He who does not punish evil commands it to be done!"

The fourth argument against the judicious practice of spanking comes from those who see it as damaging to the dignity and self-worth of the child. This subject is so important that an entire chapter has been devoted to preserving the spirit (see Chapter 4). Suffice it to say at this point that a child is fully capable of discerning whether his parent is conveying love or hatred. This is why the youngster who knows he deserves a spanking appears almost relieved when it finally comes. Rather than being insulted by the discipline, he understands its purpose and appreciates the control it gives him over his own impulses.

This childish comprehension was beautifully illustrated by a father who told me of a time when his five-year-old son was disobeying in a restaurant. This lad was sassing his mother, flipping water on his younger brother, and deliberately making a nuisance of himself. After four warnings which went unheeded, the father took his son by the arm and marched him to the parking lot where he proceeded to administer a spanking. Watching this episode was a meddling woman who had followed them out of the restaurant and into the parking lot. When the punishment began, she shook her finger at the father and screamed, "Leave that boy alone! Turn him loose! If you don't stop I'm going to call the police!" The five-year-old, who had been crying and jumping, immediately stopped yelling and said to his father in surprise, "What's wrong with that woman, Dad?" He understood the purpose for the discipline, even if the "rescuer" didn't. I only wish that Dr. Valusek and his contemporaries were as perceptive as this child.

Let me hasten to emphasize that corporal punishment is not the only tool for use in shaping the will, nor is it appropriate at all ages and for all situations. The wise parent must understand the physical and emotional characteristics of each stage in childhood, and then fit the discipline to a boy's or girl's individual needs. Perhaps I can assist in that process now by listing specific age categories and offering a few practical suggestions and examples for the various time frames. Please understand that this discussion is by no means exhaustive, and merely suggests the general nature of disciplinary methods at specific periods.

Birth to Seven Months

No *direct* discipline is necessary for a child under seven months of age, regardless of behavior or circumstance. Many parents do not agree, and find themselves "swatting" a child of six months for wiggling while being diapered or for crying in the midnight hours. This is a serious mistake. A baby is incapable of comprehending his "offense" or associating it with the resulting punishment. At this early age, he needs to be held, loved, and most important, to hear a soothing human voice. He should be fed when hungry and kept clean and dry and warm. In essence, it is probable that the foundation for emotional and physical health is laid during this first six-month period, which should be characterized by security, affection, and warmth.

On the other hand, it is possible to create a fussy, demanding baby by rushing to pick him up every time he utters a whimper or sigh. Infants are fully capable of learning to manipulate their parents through a process called reinforcement, whereby any behavior that produces a pleasant result will tend to recur. Thus, a healthy baby can keep his mother hopping around his nursery twelve hours a day (or night) by simply forcing air past his sandpaper larynx. To avoid this consequence, it is important to strike a balance between giving your baby the attention he needs and establishing him as a tiny dictator. Don't be afraid to let him cry a reasonable period of time (which is thought to be healthy for the lungs) although it is necessary to listen to the tone of his voice for the difference between random discontent and genuine distress. Most mothers learn to recognize this distinction in time.

Before leaving this first age category, I feel I must say again what has been implied before: Yes, Virginia, there *are* easy babies and there are difficult babies! Some seem determined to dismantle the homes into which they were born; they sleep cozily during the day and then howl in protest all night; they get colic and spit up the vilest stuff on their clothes (usually on the way to church); they control their internal plumbing until you hand them to strangers, and then let it blast. Instead of cuddling into the fold of the arms when being held, they stiffen rigidly in search of freedom. And to be honest, a mother may find herself leaning sockeyed over a vibrating crib at 3 A.M., asking the eternal question, "What's it all about, Alfie?"* A few days earlier she was wondering, "Will he survive?" Now she is asking, "Will *I* survive?!" But believe it or not, both generations will probably recover and this disruptive beginning will be nothing but a dim memory for the parents in such a brief moment. And from that demanding tyrant will grow a thinking, loving human being with an eternal soul and a special place in the heart of the Creator. To the exhausted and harassed new mother, let me say, "Hang tough! You are doing *the* most important job in the universe!"

* Someone has suggested that babies be fed a combination of oatmeal and garlic for dinner each evening. The stuff tastes terrible, of course, but it does help parents locate their kids in the dark! (Please don't take this suggestion literally.)

Eight to Fourteen Months

Many children will begin to test the authority of their parents during the second seven-month period. The confrontations will be minor and infrequent before the first birthday, yet the beginnings of future struggles can be seen. My own daughter, for example, challenged her mother for the first time when she was nine months old. My wife was waxing the kitchen floor when Danae crawled to the edge of the linoleum. Shirley said, "No, Danae," gesturing to the child not to enter the kitchen. Since our daughter began talking very early, she clearly understood the meaning of the word *no*. Nevertheless, she crawled straight onto the sticky wax. Shirley picked her up and sat her down in the doorway, while saying, "No," more firmly. Not to be discouraged, Danae scrambled onto the newly mopped floor. My wife took her back, saying, "No" even more strongly as she put her down. Seven times this process was repeated, until Danae finally yielded and crawled away in tears. As far as we can recall, that was the first direct collision of wills between my daughter and wife. Many more were to follow.

How does a parent discipline a one-year-old? Very carefully and gently! A child at this age is extremely easy to distract and divert. Rather than jerking a china cup from his hands, show him a brightly colored alternative—and then be prepared to catch the cup when it falls. When unavoidable confrontations do occur, as with Danae on the waxy floor, win them by firm persistence but not by punishment. Again, don't be afraid of the child's tears, which can become a potent weapon to avoid naptime or bedtime or diapertime. Have the courage to lead the child without being harsh or mean or gruff.

Compared to the months that are to follow, the period

around one year of age is usually a tranquil, smooth-functioning time in a child's life.

Fifteen to Twenty-four Months

It has been said that all human beings can be classified into two broad categories: those who would vote "yes" to the various propositions of life, and those who would be inclined to vote "no." I can tell you with confidence that each toddler around the world would definitely cast a negative vote! If there is one word that characterizes the period between fifteen and twenty-four months of age, it is *No!* No, he doesn't want to eat his cereal. No, he doesn't want to play with his dump truck. No, he doesn't want to take his bath. And you can be sure, no, he doesn't want to go to bed anytime at all. It is easy to see why this period of life has been called "the first adolescence," because of the negativism, conflict, and defiance of the age.

Dr. T. Berry Brazelton has written a beautiful description of the "terrible twos" in his excellent book *Toddlers and Parents.* (I enthusiastically recommend this book to anyone wanting to understand this fascinating and challenging age.) Quoted below is a classic depiction of a typical eighteen month old boy named Greg.[3] Although I have never met the fellow, I know him well . . . as you will when your child becomes a toddler.

> When Greg began to be negative in the second year, his parents felt as if they had been hit with a sledge hammer. His good nature seemed submerged under a load of negatives. When his parents asked anything of him, his mouth took on a grim set, his eyes narrowed, and, facing them squarely with his penetrating look, he replied simply "no!" When offered ice cream, which he loved, he preceded his acceptance with a

"no." While he rushed to get his snowsuit to go outside, he said "no" to going out.

His parents' habit of watching Greg for cues now began to turn sour. He seemed to be fighting with them all of the time. When he was asked to perform a familiar chore, his response was, "I can't." When his mother tried to stop him from emptying his clothes drawer, his response was, "I have to." He pushed hard on every familiar imposed limit, and never seemed satisfied until his parent collapsed in defeat. He would turn on the television set when his mother left the room. When she returned, she turned it off, scolded Greg mildly, and left again. He turned it on. She came rushing back to reason with him, to ask him why he'd disobeyed her. He replied, "I have to." The intensity of her insistence that he leave it alone increased. He looked steadily back at her. She returned to the kitchen. He turned it on. She was waiting behind the door, swirled in to slap his hands firmly. He sighed deeply and said, "I have to." She sat down beside him, begging him to listen to her to avoid real punishment. Again he presented a dour mask with knitted brows to her, listening but not listening. She rose wearily, walked out again. Just as wearily, he walked over to the machine to turn it on. As she came right back, tears in her eyes, to spank him, she said, "Greg, why do you want me to spank you? I hate it!" To which he replied, "I have to." As she crumpled in her chair, weeping softly with him across her lap, Greg reached up to touch her wet face.

After this clash, Mrs. Lang was exhausted. Greg sensed this and began to try to be helpful. He ran to the kitchen to fetch her mop and her dustpan, which he dragged in to her as she sat in her chair. This reversal made her smile and she gathered him up in a hug.

Greg caught her change in mood and danced off gaily to a corner, where he slid behind a chair, saying "hi and see." As he pushed the chair out, he tipped over a lamp which went crashing to the floor. His mother's reaction was a loud "No, Greg!" He curled up on the floor, his hands over his ears, eyes tightly closed, as if he were trying to shut out all the havoc he had wrought.

As soon as he was put into his high chair, he began to whine. She was so surprised that she stopped preparation of his food, and took him to change him. This did not settle the issue, and when she brought him to his chair again, he began to squirm and twist. She let him down to play until his lunch was ready. He lay on the floor, alternately whining and screeching. So unusual was this that she felt his diaper for pins which might be unclasped, felt his forehead for fever and wondered whether to give him an aspirin. Finally, she returned to fixing his lunch. Without an audience Greg subsided.

When she placed him in his chair again, his shrill whines began anew. She placed his plate in front of him with cubes of food to spear with his fork. He tossed the implement overboard, and began to push his plate away, refusing the food. Mrs. Lang was nonplussed, decided he didn't feel well, and offered him his favorite ice cream. Again, he sat helpless, refusing to feed himself. When she offered him some of the mush, he submissively allowed himself to be fed a few spoonfuls. Then he knocked the spoon out of her hand and pushed the ice cream away. Mrs. Lang was sure he was ill.

Mrs. Lang extracted Greg from his embattled position, and placed him on the floor to play while she ate her own lunch. This, of course, wasn't what he wanted either. He continued to tease her, asking for food off her plate, which he devoured greedily. His eagerness disproved her theory of illness. When she ignored him and continued to eat, his efforts redoubled. He climbed under the sink to find the bleach bottle which he brought to her on command. He fell forward onto the floor and cried loudly as if he'd hurt himself. He began to grunt as if he were having a bowel movement and to pull on his pants. This was almost a sure way of drawing his mother away from her own activity, for she'd started trying to "catch" him and put him on the toilet. This was one of his signals for her attention, and she rushed him to the toilet. He smiled smugly at her, but refused to perform. Mrs. Lang felt as if she were suddenly embattled on all fronts—none of which she could win.

When she turned to her own chores, Greg produced the bowel movement he'd been predicting.

The picture sounds pretty bleak, and admittedly, there are times when a little toddler can dismantle the peace and tranquillity of a home. (My son Ryan loved to blow bubbles in the dog's water dish—a game which still horrifies me.) However, with all of its struggles, there is no more thrilling time of life than this period of dynamic blossoming and unfolding. New words are being learned daily, and the cute verbal expressions of that age will be remembered for a half century. It is a time of excitement over fairy stories and Santa Claus and furry puppy dogs. And most important, it is a precious time of loving and warmth that will scurry by all too quickly. There are millions of older parents today with grown children who would give all they possess to relive those bubbly days with their toddlers.

Let me make a few disciplinary recommendations which will, I hope, ease some of the tension of the toddler experience. I must hasten to say, however, that the negativism of this turbulent period is both normal and healthy, and *nothing* will make an eighteen-month-old child act like a five-year-old.

First, and for obvious reasons, it is extremely important to fathers to help discipline and participate in the parenting process when possible. Children need their fathers and respond to their masculine manner, of course, but wives need their husbands, too. This is especially true of housewives, such as Greg's mother, who have done combat duty through the long day and find themselves in a state of battle fatigue by nightfall. Husbands get tired too, of course, but if they can hold together long enough to help get the little tigers in bed, nothing could contribute more to the stability of their homes. I am especially sympathetic with the mother who is raising a toddler or two and an infant at the same time. There is no more difficult assignment on the face of the earth. Husbands who recognize this fact can help their wives feel understood, loved and supported in the vital jobs they are doing. (Don't ask me, please, how to convince husbands to accept that responsibility. I'm like the mouse who recommended that a bell be put around the neck of the cat, but had no idea how to get it there!)

With regard to specific discipline of the strong-willed toddler, mild spankings can begin between fifteen and eighteen months of age. They should be relatively infrequent, and must be reserved for the kind of defiance Greg displayed over the television set. He clearly knew what his mother wanted, but refused to comply. He should *not* have been spanked for knocking over the lamp or for the bowel movement episode or for refusing to eat his ice cream. A heavy hand of authority during this period causes the child to suppress his need to experiment and test his environment, which can have long lasting consequences. To repeat, the toddler should be taught to obey and yield to parental leadership, but that end result will not be accomplished overnight.

When spankings occur, they should be administered with a neutral object; that is, with a small switch or belt, but rarely with the hand. I have always felt that the hand should be seen by the child as an object of love rather than an instrument of punishment. Furthermore, if a parent commonly slaps a youngster when he is not expecting to be hit, then he will probably duck and flinch whenever Father suddenly scratches his ear. And, of course, a slap in the face can reposition the nose or do permanent damage to the ears or jaw. If all spankings are administered with a neutral object, applied where intended, then the child need never fear that he will suddenly be chastised for some accidental indiscretion. (There are exceptions to this rule, such as when a child's hands are slapped or thumped for reaching for a stove or other dangerous object.) Incidentally, I mentioned in *Dare to Discipline* that my mother once spanked me with a girdle for being sassy and rude. One man read that story and became so angry that he refused to come and hear me speak the next time I was in his city. I found out later why he was so incensed. He had misread my explanation and thought my mother had hit me with a griddle! There is a difference between the two, although girdles in 1940 weighed about sixteen pounds and were riveted with steel bolts down both sides. It was also equipped with dozens of straps and buckles that dangled ominously from the bottom. In some ways, a griddle would have been easier to duck than this abominable undergarment which was flung in my direction.

Should a spanking hurt? Yes, or else it will have no influence. A swat on the behind through three layers of wet diapers simply conveys no urgent message. However, a small amount of pain for a young child goes a long way; it is certainly not necessary to lash or "whip" him. Two or three stinging strokes on the legs or bottom with a switch are usually sufficient to emphasize the point, "You must obey me." And finally, it is important to spank *immediately* after the offense, or not at all. A toddler's memory is not sufficiently developed to permit even a ten-minute delay in the administration of justice. Then after the episode is over and the tears subsided, the child might want to be held and reassured by his mother or father. By all means, let him come. Embrace him in the security of your loving arms. Rock him softly. Tell him how much you love him and why he must "mind his mommie." This moment can be the most important event in the entire day.

I caution parents not to punish toddlers for behavior which is natural and necessary to learning and development. Exploration of their environment, for example, is of great importance to intellectual stimulation. You and I as adults will look at a crystal trinket and obtain whatever information we seek from that visual inspection. A toddler, however, will expose it to all of his senses. He will pick it up, taste it, smell it, wave it in the air, pound it on the wall, throw it across the room, and listen to the pretty sound that it makes when shattering. By that process he learns a bit about gravity, rough versus smooth surfaces, the brittle nature of glass, and some startling things about mother's anger.

Am I suggesting that children be allowed to destroy a home and all of its contents? No, but neither is it right to expect a curious child to keep his hands to himself. Parents should remove those items that are fragile or particularly dangerous, and then strew the child's path with fascinating objects of all types. Permit him to explore everything possible and do not ever punish him for touching something that he *did not know was off limits,* regardless of its value. With respect to dangerous items, such as electric plugs and stoves, as well as a few untouchable objects, such as the knobs on the television set, it is possible and necessary to teach and enforce the command, "Don't touch!" After making it clear what is expected, a thump on the fingers or slap on the hands will usually discourage repeat episodes.

Entire books have been written on the subject which I have only touched here. Nevertheless, I hope this brief introduction will give the "flavor" of discipline for the young toddler.

Before leaving this dynamic time of life, I must share with my readers the results of an extremely important ten-year study of children between eight and eighteen months of age. This investigation, known as Harvard University's Preschool Project, has been guided by Dr. Burton L. White and a team of fifteen researchers between 1965 and 1975. They studied young children intensely during this period, hoping to discover which experiences in the early years of life contribute to the development of a healthy, intelligent human being. The conclusions from this exhaustive effort are summarized below, as reported originally in the *APA Monitor.*[4]

1. It is increasingly clear that the origins of human competence are to be found in a critical period of development between eight and eighteen months of age. The child's experiences during these brief months do more to influence future intellectual competence than any time before or after.

2. The single most important environmental factor in the life of the child is his mother. "She is on the hook," said Dr. White, and carries more influence on her child's experiences than any other person or circumstance.

3. The amount of *live* language directed to a child (not to be confused with television, radio, or overheard conversations) is vital to his development of fundamental linguistic, intellectual, and social skills. The researchers concluded, "Providing a rich social life for a twelve- to fifteen-month-old child is the best thing you can do to guarantee a good mind."

4. Those children who are given free access to living areas of their homes progressed much faster than those whose movements are restricted.

5. The nuclear family is the most important educational delivery system. If we are going to produce capable, healthy children, it will be by strengthening family units and by improving the interactions that occur within them.

6. The best parents were those who excelled at three key functions:
   (1) They were superb designers and organizers of their children's environments.
   (2) They permitted their children to interrupt them for brief thirty-second episodes, during

which personal consultation, comfort, information, and enthusiasm were exchanged.

(3) "THEY WERE FIRM DISCIPLINARIANS
WHILE SIMULTANEOUSLY SHOWING
GREAT AFFECTION FOR THEIR CHIL-
DREN." (I couldn't have said it better my-
self.)

Do these results speak dramatically to anyone but me?
I hear within them an affirmation and validation of the
concepts to which I have devoted my professional life.

Two to Three Years

Perhaps the most frustrating aspect of the "terrible twos"
is the tendency of kids to spill things, destroy things, eat
horrible things, fall off things, flush things, kill things, and
get into things. They also have a knack for doing embarrassing things, like sneezing on a nearby man at a lunch
counter. During these toddler years, any unexplained silence of more than thirty seconds can throw an adult into
a sudden state of panic. What mother has not had the thrill
of opening the bedroom door, only to find Tony Tornado
covered with lipstick from the top of his pink head to the
carpet on which he stands? On the wall is his own artistic
creation with a red handprint in the center, and throughout the room is the aroma of Chanel No. 5 with which he
has anointed his baby brother. Wouldn't it be interesting to
hold a national convention sometime, bringing together all
the mothers who have experienced that exact trauma?

When my daughter was two years of age, she was fascinated the first time she watched me shave in the morning.
She stood captivated as I soaped my face and began using

the razor. That should have been my first clue that something was up. The following morning, Shirley came into the bathroom to find our dachshund, Siggie, sitting in his favorite spot on the furry lid of the toilet seat. Danae had covered his head with lather and was systematically shaving the hair from his shiny skull! Shirley screamed, "Danae!" which sent Siggie and his barber scurrying for safety. It was a strange sight to see the frightened dog with nothing but ears sticking up on the top of his bald head.

When Ryan was the same age, he had an incredible ability to make messes. He could turn it over or spill it faster than any kid I've ever seen, especially at meal time. (Once while eating a peanut butter sandwich he thrust his hand through the bottom side. When his fingers emerged at the top they were covered with peanut butter, and Ryan didn't recognize them. The poor lad nearly bit off his index finger.) Because of his destructive inclination, Ryan heard the word "mess" used repeatedly by his parents. It became one of the most important words in his vocabulary. One evening while taking a shower I left the door ajar and got some water on the floor. And as you might expect, Ryan came thumping around the corner and stepped in it. He looked up at me and said in the gruffest voice he could manage, "Whuss all this mess in hyere?"

You *must* keep a sense of humor during the twos and threes in order to preserve your own sanity. But you must also proceed with the task of instilling obedience and respect for authority. Thus, most of the comments written in the preceding section also apply to the child between twenty-two and thirty-six months of age. Although the "older" toddler is much different physically and emotionally than he was at eighteen months, the tendency to test and challenge parental authority is still very much in evidence. In fact, when the young toddler consistently wins the early

confrontations and conflicts, he becomes even more difficult
to handle in the second and third years. Then a lifelong
disrespect for authority often begins to settle into his young
mind. Therefore, I cannot overemphasize the importance of
instilling two distinct messages within your child before he
is forty-eight months of age: (1) "I love you more than
you can possibly understand. You are precious to me and
I thank God every day that He let me raise you!" (2) "Because I love you, I must teach you to obey me. That is the
only way I can take care of you and protect you from things
that might hurt you. Let's read what the Bible tells us:
'Children, obey your parents, for this is what God wants
you to do.' " (Ephesians 6:1)

Healthy parenthood can be boiled down to those two essential ingredients, love and control, operating in a system
of checks and balances. Any concentration on love to the
exclusion of control usually breeds disrespect and contempt. Conversely, an authoritarian and oppressive home
atmosphere is deeply resented by the child who feels un-
loved or even hated. To repeat, the objective for the toddler years is to strike a balance between mercy and justice,
affection and authority, love and control.

Specifically, how does one discipline a "naughty" two- or
three-year-old child? One possible approach is to require
the boy or girl to sit in a chair and think about what he
has done. Most children of this age are bursting with
energy, and absolutely hate to spend ten dull minutes with
their wiggly posteriors glued to a chair. To some individuals, this form of punishment can be even more effective
than a spanking, and is remembered longer.

Parents to whom I have made that recommendation have
often said, "But what if he won't stay in the chair?" The
same question is asked with reference to the child's tendency to pop out of bed after being tucked in at night. These

are examples of the direct confrontations I have been describing. The parent who cannot require a toddler to stay
on a chair or in his bed is not yet in command of the child.
There is no better time than now to change the relationship.

I would suggest that the youngster be placed in bed and
given a little speech, such as, "Johnny, this time Mommie
means business. Are you listening to me? *Do not* get out
of this bed. Do you understand me?" Then when Johnny's
feet touch the floor, give him one swat on the legs with a
small switch. Put the switch on his dresser where he can
see it, and promise him one more stroke if he gets up
again. Walk confidently out of the room without further
comment. If he rebounds again, fulfill your promise and
offer the same warning if he doesn't stay in bed. Repeat the
episode until Johnny acknowledges that you are the boss.
Then hug him, tell him you love him, and remind him how
important it is for him to get his rest so that he won't be
sick, etc. Your purpose in this painful exercise (painful for
both parties) is not only to keep li'l John in bed, but to
confirm your leadership in his mind. It is my opinion that
too many American parents lack the courage to win this
kind of confrontation, and are off-balance and defensive
ever after. Dr. Benjamin Spock wrote in 1974, "Inability
to be firm is, to my mind, the commonest problem of parents in America today." I agree.

Four to Eight Years

By the time a child reaches four years of age, the focus
of discipline should be not only on his behavior, but also
on the *attitudes* which motivate it. This task of shaping the
personality can be relatively simple or incredibly difficult,
depending on the basic temperament of a particular child.

Some youngsters are naturally warm and loving and trusting, while others sincerely believe the world is out to get them. Some enjoy giving and sharing, whereas their siblings are consistently selfish and demanding. Some smile throughout the day while others complain and bellyache about everything from toothpaste to turnip greens.

Furthermore, these attitudinal patterns are not consistent from one time to the next. They tend to alternate cyclically between rebellion and obedience. In other words, a time of intense conflict and defiance (if properly handled) gives way to a period of love and cooperation. Then when Mom and Dad relax and congratulate themselves for doing a super job of parenting, their little chameleon changes colors again.

Some might ask, "So what? Why should we be concerned about the attitudes of a boy or girl?" Indeed, there are many child-rearing specialists who suggest that parents ignore negative attitudes, including those which are unmistakably defiant in tone. Consider the naive recommendations of Dr. Luther Woodward, as paraphrased in the book for parents, *Your Child from Two to Five.*

> What do you do when your preschooler calls you a "big stinker" or threatens to flush you down the toilet? Do you scold, punish . . . or sensibly take it in your stride? . . .
>
> Dr. Woodward recommends a positive policy of understanding as the best and fastest way to help a child outgrow this verbal violence. When parents fully realize that all little tots feel angry and destructive at times, they are better able to minimize these outbursts. Once the preschooler gets rid of his hostility, the desire to destroy is gone and instinctive feelings of love and affection have a chance to sprout and grow. Once

the child is six or seven, parents can rightly let the child know that he is expected to be outgrowing sassing his parents.

In conclusion, Dr. Woodward reveals the permissive implications of his recommendation by warning those who try to apply it:

> But this policy takes a broad perspective and a lot of composure, especially when friends and relatives voice disapproval and warn you that you are bringing up a brat.[5]

In this case, your friends and relatives will probably be right. This suggestion (published during the permissive 1950s and so typical of other writings from that era) is based on the simplistic notion that children will develop sweet and loving attitudes if we adults will permit and encourage their temper tantrums during childhood. According to the optimistic Dr. Woodward, the tot who has been calling his mother a "big stinker" for six or seven years can be expected to embrace her suddenly in love and dignity. That outcome is most improbable. Dr. Woodward's creative "policy of understanding" (which means, stand and do nothing) offers a one-way ticket to emotional and social disaster, in my view.

I expressed my contrasting opinion in my earlier book *Dare to Discipline:*

> If it is desirable that children be kind, appreciative, and pleasant, those qualities should be taught—not hoped for. If we want to see honesty, truthfulness, and unselfishness in our offspring, then these characteristics should be the conscious objectives of our early

instructional process. If it is important to produce respectful, responsible young citizens, then we should set out to mold them accordingly.

The point is obvious: heredity does not equip a child with proper attitudes; children will learn what they are taught. We cannot expect the desirable attitudes and behavior to appear if we have not done our early homework. It seems clear that many of the parents of the post-war crop of American babies failed in that critical assignment.[6]

But *how* does one shape the attitudes of children? Most parents find it easier to deal with outright disobedience than with unpleasant characteristics of temperament or personality. Let me restate two age-old suggestions for parents, and then I'll offer a system which can be used with the especially disagreeable child.

1. There is no substitute for parental modeling of the attitudes we wish to teach. Someone wrote, "The footsteps a child follows are most likely to be the ones his parents thought they covered up." It is true. Our children are watching us carefully, and they instinctively imitate our behavior. Therefore, we can hardly expect them to be kind and giving if we are consistently grouchy and selfish. We will be unable to teach appreciativeness if we never say "please" or "thank you" at home or abroad. We will not produce honest children if we teach them to lie to the bill collector on the phone by saying, "Dad's not home." In these matters, our boys and girls instantly discern the gap between what we say and what we do. And of the two choices, they usually identify with our behavior and ignore our empty proclamations.

2. Most of the favorable attitudes which should be taught are actually extrapolations of the Judeo-Christian ethic, including honesty, respect, kindness, love, human dignity, obedience, responsibility, reverence, etc. And how are these time-honored principles conveyed to the next generation? The answer was provided by Moses as he wrote more than 4000 years ago in the book of Deuteronomy. "You must teach them to your children and talk about them when you are at home or out for a walk; at bedtime, and the first thing in the morning. Tie them on your finger, wear them on your forehead, and write them on the doorposts of your house." (Deut. 6:7–9, TLB) In other words, we can't instill these attitudes during a brief, two-minute bedtime prayer, or during formalized training sessions. We must *live* them from morning to night. They should be reinforced during our casual conversation, being punctuated with illustrations, demonstrations, compliments, and chastisement. This teaching task is, I believe, *the* most important assignment God has given to us as parents.

Finally, let me offer a suggested approach for use with the strong-willed or negative child (age six or older) for whom other forms of instruction have been ineffective. I am referring specifically to the sour, complaining child who is making himself and the rest of the family miserable. He may slide his brakes for weeks and criticize the efforts of everyone nearby. The problem with such an individual is in defining the changes that are desired and then reinforcing the improvements when they occur. Attitudes are abstractions that a six- or eight-year-old may not fully understand, and we need a system that will clarify the "target" in his mind.

Toward this end, I have developed an Attitude Chart (see illustration) which translates these subtle mannerisms into concrete mathematical terms. Please note: This system

MY ATTITUDE CHART _____
DATE

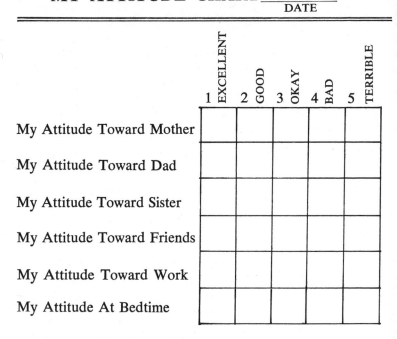

	1 EXCELLENT	2 GOOD	3 OKAY	4 BAD	5 TERRIBLE
My Attitude Toward Mother					
My Attitude Toward Dad					
My Attitude Toward Sister					
My Attitude Toward Friends					
My Attitude Toward Work					
My Attitude At Bedtime					

TOTAL POINTS _____

CONSEQUENCES

6–9 POINTS	THE FAMILY WILL DO SOMETHING FUN TOGETHER
10–18 POINTS	NOTHING HAPPENS, GOOD OR BAD
19–20 POINTS	I HAVE TO STAY IN MY ROOM FOR ONE HOUR
21–22 POINTS	I GET ONE SWAT WITH BELT
23+ POINTS	I GET TWO SWATS WITH BELT

which follows would *not* be appropriate for the child who merely has a bad day, or displays temporary unpleasantness associated with illness, fatigue, or environmental circumstances. Rather, it is a remedial tool to help change persistently negative and disrespectful attitudes by making the child conscious of his problem.

The Attitude Chart should be prepared and then reproduced, since a separate sheet will be needed every day. Place an X in the appropriate square for each category, and then add the total points "earned" by bedtime. Although this nightly evaluation process has the appearance of being objective to a child, it is obvious that the parent can influence the outcome by considering it in advance (it's called cheating). Mom or Dad may want Junior to receive eighteen points on the first night, barely missing the punishment but realizing he must stretch the following day. I must emphasize, however, that the system will fail miserably if a naughty child does not receive the punishment he deserves, or if he hustles to improve but does not obtain the family fun he was promised. This approach is nothing more than a method of applying reward and punishment to attitudes in a way that children can understand and remember.

For the child who does not fully comprehend the concept of numbers, it might be helpful to plot the daily totals on a cumulative graph, such as the one provided below.

I don't expect everyone to appreciate this system or to apply it at home. In fact, parents of compliant, happy children will be puzzled as to why it would ever be needed. However, the mothers and fathers of sullen, ill-tempered children will comprehend more quickly. Take it or leave it, as the situation warrants.

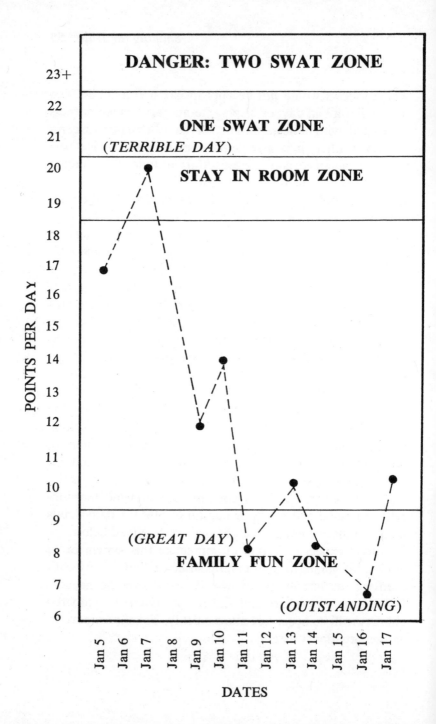

Nine to Twelve Years

Ideally, the foundation has been laid during the first nine years which will then permit a general loosening of the lines of authority. Every year that passes should bring fewer rules, less direct discipline, and more independence for the child. This does not mean that a ten-year-old is suddenly emancipated; it does mean that he is permitted to make more decisions about his daily living than when he was six. It also means that he should be carrying more responsibility each year of his life.

Physical punishment should be relatively infrequent during this period immediately prior to adolescence. Of course, some strong-willed children absolutely demand to be spanked, and their wishes should be granted. However, the compliant youngster should have experienced his last woodshed episode by the end of his first decade (or even four years earlier).

The overall objective during this final preadolescent period is to teach the child that his actions have inevitable consequences. One of the most serious casualties in a permissive society is the failure to connect those two factors, behavior and consequences. Too often, a three-year-old child screams insults at his mother, but Mom stands blinking her eyes in confusion. A first-grader launches an attack on his teacher, but the school makes allowances for his age and takes no action. A ten-year-old is caught stealing candy in a store, but is released to the recognizance of his parents. A fifteen-year-old sneaks the keys to the family car, but his father pays the fine when he is arrested. A seventeen-year-old drives his Chevy like a maniac and his parents pay for the repairs when he wraps it around a telephone pole. You see, all through childhood, loving parents seem determined to intervene between behavior and consequences, breaking the connection and preventing the valuable learning that could have occurred.

Thus, it is possible for a young man or woman to enter adult life, not really knowing that life bites—that every move we make directly affects our future—that irresponsible behavior eventually produces sorrow and pain. Such a person applies for his first job and arrives late for work three times during the first week; then, when he is fired in a flurry of hot words, he becomes bitter and frustrated. It was the first time in his life that Mom and Dad couldn't come running to rescue him from the unpleasant consequences. (Unfortunately, many American parents still try to "bail out" their grown children even when they are in their twenties and live away from home.) What is the result? This overprotection produces emotional cripples who often develop lasting characteristics of dependency and a kind of perpetual adolescence.

How does one connect behavior with consequences? By being willing to let the child experience a reasonable amount of pain when he behaves irresponsibly. When Jack misses the school bus through his own dawdling, let him walk a mile or two and enter school in midmorning (unless safety factors prevent this). If Janie carelessly loses her lunch money, let her skip a meal. Obviously, it is possible to carry this principle too far, being harsh and inflexible with an immature child. But the best approach is to expect boys and girls to carry the responsibility that is appropriate for their age, and occasionally to taste the bitter fruit that irresponsibility bears.

Let me offer a concluding illustration that may be read to an eleven- or twelve-year-old child. The following story was published by United Press International a few days after an eclipse of the sun had occurred.[7]

'JUST KEPT STARING'
'I WAS FASCINATED,' GIRL SAYS
OF ECLIPSE—NOW SHE'S BLIND

TIPTON, Ind. (UPI)—Ann Turner, 15, is living proof of the danger of trying to watch a solar eclipse with the naked eye. Now she is blind.

On March 7, despite the warnings she had read, Ann "took a quick look through the window" at her home at the solar eclipse in progress.

"For some reason, I just kept staring out of the window," she told Pat Cline, a reporter for the Tipton Daily Tribune. "I was fascinated by what was taking place in the sky.

"There was no pain or feeling of discomfort as I watched. I stood there perhaps four or five minutes when mom caught me and made me turn away from the window."

Ann said she "saw spots before my eyes but I didn't think much about it." Shortly afterward, she walked downtown and suddenly realized when she looked at a traffic signal that she could not read signs.

Frightened, Ann turned around and headed home. As she neared the porch, she said, she found she was "walking in darkness."

She was too scared to tell her family until the next day, although she "had an intuition or suspicion that something terrible was happening."

"I cried and cried," she said. "I didn't want to be blind. God knows I didn't want to live in darkness the rest of my life.

"I kept hoping the nightmare would end and I could see again but the darkness kept getting worse. I was scared. I had disobeyed my parents and the other warnings. I could not go back and change things. It was too late."

When Mr. and Mrs. Coy Turner learned what had happened, they took Ann to specialists. But the doctors shook their heads and said they could not help Ann regain her sight. They said she is 90% blind and can make out only faint lines of large objects on the periphery of what used to be her normal sight field.

With the help of a tutor, Ann is going ahead with her education. She is learning to adjust to the world of darkness.

After reading this dramatic story to your boy or girl, it might be wise to say, "Paul, this terrible thing happened to Ann because she didn't believe what she was told by her parents and other adults. She trusted her own judgment, instead. And the reason I read this to you is to help you understand that you might soon be in a situation that is similar to Ann's. As you go into your teen years, you will have many opportunities to do some things that we have told you are harmful. For example, someone could give you some drugs which don't seem dangerous at all, even after you take them. Just like Ann, you may not realize the consequences until it is too late. That is why it will be so important for you to *believe* the warnings that you've been taught, rather than trust your own judgment. Many young people make mistakes during the teen-age years that will affect the rest of their lives, and I want to help you avoid those problems. But the truth of the matter is, only you can set your course and choose your pathway. You can accept what your eyes tell you, like Ann, or you can believe what your mother and I have said, and more important, what we read in God's Word. I have confidence that you will make the right decisions, and it's going to be fun watching you grow up."

There is so much that should be said about this late childhood era, but time and space limitations force me to move on. In conclusion, the period between ten and eleven years of age often represents a final time of great closeness and unpretentious love between parent and child. Enjoy it to the maximum, for believe me, there are more tumultuous days coming! (I have chosen to reserve the discussion of adolescent discipline for a separate chapter, because of the significance of the topic.)

Final Comment

I was accompanied on a recent speaking trip by my wife, Shirley, which required us to leave our two children with their grandparents for a full week. My wife's mother and father are wonderful people and dearly love Danae and Ryan. However, two bouncing, jumping, giggling little rascals can wear down the nerves of *any* adult, especially those who are approaching the age of retirement. When we returned home from the trip I asked my father-in-law how the children behaved and whether or not they caused him any problems. He replied in his North Dakota (Lawrence Welk) accent, "Oh no! Dere good kids. But the important thing is, you jus' got to keep 'em out in da open."

That was probably the best disciplinary advice ever offered. Many behavioral problems can be prevented by simply avoiding the circumstances that create them. And especially for boys and girls growing up in our congested cities, perhaps what we need most is to "get 'em out in da open." It's not a bad idea.

QUESTIONS

Question: Isn't it our goal to produce children with *self*-discipline and *self*-reliance? If so, how does your approach to *external* discipline by parents get translated into internal control?

Answer: You've asked a provocative question, but one that reveals a misunderstanding of children, I believe. There are many authorities who suggest that parents not discipline their children for the reason implied by your question: they want their kids to discipline themselves. But since young people lack the maturity to generate that self-control, they stumble through childhood without experiencing *either* internal or external discipline. Thus, they enter adult life having never completed an unpleasant assignment, or accepted an order that they disliked, or yielded to the leadership of their elders. Can we expect such a person to exercise self-discipline in young adulthood? I think not. He doesn't even know the meaning of the word.

My concept is that parents should introduce their child to discipline and self-control by the use of external influences when he is young. By being required to behave responsibly, he gains valuable experience in controlling his *own* impulses and resources. Then as he grows into the teen years, the transfer of responsibility is made year by year from the shoulders of the parent directly to the child. He is no longer forced to do what he has learned during earlier years. To illustrate, a child should be *required* to keep his room relatively neat when he is young. Then somewhere during the midteens, his own self-discipline should take over and provide the motivation to continue the task. If it does not, the parent should close his door and let him live in a dump, if necessary.

Question: I'm never completely certain how to react to the behavior of my children. Can you give some specific examples of misbehaviors that should be punished, as well as others which can be ignored or handled differently?

Answer: Certainly. Let me list a few examples at various age levels, asking you to decide how you would handle each matter before reading my suggestions. (Most of these items represent actual situations posed to me by parents.)

1. I get very upset because my two-year-old boy will not sit still and be quiet in church. He knows he's not supposed to be noisy, but he hits his toys on the pew and sometimes talks out loud. Should I spank him for being so disruptive?

My reply

The mother who wrote this question during one of my seminars revealed a poor understanding of toddlers. Most two-year-olds can no more fold their hands and sit quietly in church than they could swim the Atlantic Ocean. They squirm and churn and burn every second of their waking hours. No, this child should not be punished. He should be left in the nursery where he can shake the foundations without disturbing the worshipers.

2. My four-year-old son came into the house and told me he had seen a lion in the back yard. He was not trying to be funny. He really tried to convince me that this lie was true and became quite upset when I didn't believe him. I want him to be an honest and truthful person. Should I have spanked him?

My reply

Definitely not. There is a *very* thin line between fantasy and reality in the mind of a preschool child, and he often confuses the two. This occurred when I took my son to Disneyland at three years of age. He was absolutely terrified by the wolf who stalked around with the three pigs. Ryan took one look at those sharp, jagged teeth and screamed in terror. I have a priceless motion picture of him scrambling for the safety of his mother's arms. After we returned home, I told Ryan there was a "very nice man" inside the wolf suit, who wouldn't hurt anyone. My son was so relieved by that news that he needed to hear it repeatedly.

He would say, "Dad?"

"What, Ryan?"

"Tell me 'bout that nice man!"

You see, Ryan was not able to distinguish between the fantasy character and a genuine threat to his health and safety. I would guess that the lion story related in the question above was a product of the same kind of confusion. The child may well have believed that a lion was in the back yard. This mother would have been wise to play along with the game while making it perfectly clear that she didn't believe the story. She could have said, "My! My! A lion in the back yard. I sure hope he is a friendly old cat. Now, Billy, please wash your hands and come eat lunch."

3. My six-year-old has suddenly become sassy and disrespectful in his manner at home. He told me to "buzz off" when I asked him to take out the trash, and he calls me names when he gets angry. I feel it is important to permit this emotional outlet, so I haven't suppressed it. Do you agree?

My reply

I couldn't disagree more strongly. Your son is aware of his sudden defiance, and he's waiting to see how far you will let him go. This kind of behavior, if unchecked, will continue to deteriorate day by day, producing a more profound disrespect with each encounter. If you don't discourage it, you can expect some wild experiences during the adolescent years to come. Thus, the behavior for which punishment is most necessary is that involving a direct assault on the leadership and personhood of the parent (or teacher), especially when the child obviously knows he shouldn't be acting that way.

With regard to the ventilation of anger, it is possible to let a child express his strongest feelings without being insulting or disrespectful. A tearful charge, "You weren't fair with me and you embarrassed me in front of my friends," should be accepted and responded to quietly and earnestly. But a parent should never permit a child to say, "You are so stupid and you never do anything right!" The first statement is a genuine expression of frustration based on a specific issue; the second is an attack on the dignity and authority of the parent. In my opinion, the latter is damaging to both generations and should be inhibited.

4. My ten-year-old often puts his milk glass too close to his elbow when eating, and has knocked it over at least six times. I keep telling him to move the glass, but he won't listen. When he spilt the milk again yesterday, I jerked him up and gave him a spanking with a belt. Today I don't feel good about the incident. Should I have reacted more patiently?

My reply

It is all too easy to tell a mother she shouldn't have become so upset over something that happened yesterday. After all, I'm not the one who had to clean up the mess. However, your son did not *intend* to spill his milk and he was, in effect, punished for his irresponsibility. It would have been better to create a method of grabbing his attention and helping him remember to return his glass to a safe area. For example, you could have cut an "off limits" zone from red construction paper, and taped it to the side of his plate. If junior placed his glass on that paper, he would have to help wash the dishes after the evening meal. I guarantee you that he would seldom "forget" again. In fact, this procedure would probably sensitize him to the location of the glass, even after the paper was removed.

5. John is in the second grade and is playing around in school. Last month his teacher sent home a note telling us of his misbehavior, and he threw it away. We discovered at Open House the following week that he had lied to us and destroyed the note. What would you have done?

My reply

That was a deliberate act of disobedience. After investigating the facts, I would probably have given John a spanking for his misbehavior in school and for being un-truthful to his parents. I would then talk to his teacher about *why* he was cavorting in school and consider why he was afraid to bring home the note.

6. My three-year-old daughter, Nancy, plays unpleasant games with me in grocery stores. She runs when I call her and makes demands for candy and gum and cupcakes. When I refuse, she throws the most embarrassing temper tantrums you can imagine. I don't want to punish her in front of all those people and she knows it. What should I do?

My reply

If there are sanctuaries where the usual rules and re-strictions do not apply, then your children will behave dif-ferently in those protected zones than elsewhere. I would suggest that you have a talk with Nancy on the next trip to the market. Tell her exactly what you expect, and make it clear that you mean business. Then when the same be-havior occurs, take her to the car or behind the building and do what you would have done at home. She'll get the message.

7. Our twenty-four-month-old son is not yet toilet trained, although my mother-in-law feels he should be under control now. Should we spank him for using his pants instead of the potty?

My reply

No. Tell your mother-in-law to cool down a bit. It is entirely possible that your child *can't* control himself at this age. The last thing you want to do is spank a two-year-old for an offense which he can't comprehend. If I had to err on this matter, it would be in the direction of being too late with my demands, rather than too early. Furthermore, the best approach to potty training is with rewards rather than with punishment. Give him a sucker (or sugarless candy) for performing properly. When you've proved that he can comply, then you can hold him responsible in the future.

SUMMARY

In summary, it is impossible to discipline properly until the parent is able to interpret the child's intent. Corporal punishment should occur only in response to deliberate disobedience or defiance.

"But how can you know for sure?" That question has been asked of me hundreds of times. A mother will say, "I think Chuckie was being disrespectful when I told him to take his bath, but I'm not sure what he was thinking."

There is a very straightforward solution to this parental dilemma: use the first occasion for the purpose of clarifying the next. Say to your son, "Chuck, your answer to me just now sounded sassy. I'm not sure how you intended it. But so we will understand each other, don't talk to me like that again." If it occurs again, you'll know it was deliberate.

Most confusion over how to discipline results from parents' failure to define the limits properly. If you're hazy on what is acceptable and unacceptable, then your child will be doubly confused. Therefore, don't punish until you have drawn the boundaries too clearly to be missed. Most children will then accept them with only an occasional indiscretion.

3 Protecting the Spirit

There are dangers implicit in what I have stated about discipline of the strong-willed child. The reader could assume that I perceive children as the villains and parents as the inevitable good guys. Of greater concern is the inference that I'm recommending a rigid, harsh, oppressive approach to discipline in the home. Neither statement is even partially accurate.

By contrast, I see small children (even those who challenge authority) as vulnerable little creatures who need buckets of love and tenderness every day of their lives. One of my great frustrations in teaching parents has been the difficulty in conveying a *balanced* environment, wherein discipline is evident when necessary, but where it is matched by patience and respect and affection. Let it never be said that I favor the "slap 'em across the mouth" approach to authoritarianism. That hostile manner not only wounds the spirit, but it's hard on teeth, too.

No subject distresses me more than the phenomenon of child abuse which is so prevalent in America today. There are children all across this country, even while I write, who are suffering untold miseries at the hands of their parents. Some of these pitiful little tots are brought to our hospital in every imaginable condition. They have been burned and bruised and broken and their little minds are permanently warped by the awful circumstances into which they were born.

Every professional who works with hurt children has to learn to cope with his own empathy. I have gained a measure of control over my own emotions; however, I have never been able to observe a battered child without feeling a literal agony within my chest. Diseased children suffer, of course, but most of them experience some measure of parental love which provides an emotional undergirding. But battered children suffer physically *and* emotionally. For them, no one cares. No one understands. There is no one to whom the longings can be expressed. They cannot escape. They cannot explain why they are hated. And many of them are too young to develop defense mechanisms or even call for help.

I dealt this spring with an eight-year-old girl who had been sexually assaulted repeatedly by her alcoholic father since she was fifteen months of age. What an immeasurable tragedy! Another child in Los Angeles was blinded by his mother, who destroyed his eyes with a razor blade. Can you imagine going through life knowing that your handicap resulted from a deliberate act by your own mother? Another small child in our city was pushed from a car on a crowded freeway and left clinging to the chain link divider for eight or nine hours. Another child's feet were held to a hot iron as punishment.

Less than five minutes ago, a radio news summary broadcast through my office intercom told of finding a ten-year-old girl hanging by her heels in her parents' garage. These kinds of horror stories are all too familiar to those of us who work with children. In fact, it is highly probable that some youngster within a mile or two of your house is experiencing destructive abuse in one manner or another. Brian G. Fraser, attorney for the National Center for Prevention and Treatment of Child Abuse and Neglect, has written: "Child abuse . . . once thought to be primarily a problem of the poor and down-trodden . . . occurs in every segment of society and may be the country's leading cause of death in children."

The last thing on earth that I want to do is to provide a rationalization and justification for such parental oppression. Let me say it again: I don't believe in harsh, inflexible discipline, even when it is well intentioned. Children must be given room to breathe and grow and love. But there are also threatening circumstances at the permissive end of the spectrum, and many parents fall into one trap in an earnest attempt to avoid the other. These dual dangers were beautifully described by Marguerite and Willard Beecher, writing in their book *Parents on the Run:*

> The adult-centered home of yesteryear made parents the masters and children their slaves. The child-centered home of today has made parents the slaves and children the masters. There is no true cooperation in any master-slave relationship, and therefore

no democracy. Neither the restrictive-authoritative technique of rearing children nor the newer "anything-goes" technique develop the genius within the individual, because neither trains him to be self-reliant . . .

Children reared under arbitrary rules become either spineless automatons or bitter revolutionaries who waste their lives in conflict with those around them. But children who know no law higher than their own passing fancy become trapped by their own appetites. In either case, they are slaves. The former are enslaved by leaders on whom they depend to tell them what to do, and the latter are enslaved by the pawn-broker. Neither are (sic) capable of maintaining society on any decent basis. A lifetime of unhappiness may be avoided if the twig is bent so the tree will not incline in either of these mistaken directions.[1]

But how can this be accomplished on behalf of our children? How can parents steer a course between the unpleasant alternatives of permissiveness and oppression? What philosophy will guide our efforts?

Our objective is not only to shape the will of the child, as described in the previous chapters, *but to do so without breaking his spirit*. To accomplish this purpose we must understand the characteristic difference between the will and the spirit.

As I've stated, a child's *will* is a powerful force in the human personality. It is one of the few intellectual components which arrives full strength at the moment of birth. In a recent issue of *Psychology Today*, this heading described the research findings from a study of infancy: "A baby knows who he is before he has language to tell us so. He reaches deliberately for control of his environment, especially his parents." This scientific disclosure would bring no new revelation to the parents of a strong-willed infant. They have walked the floor with him in the wee small hours, listening to this tiny dictator as he made his wants and wishes abundantly clear.

Later, a defiant toddler can become so angry that he is capable of holding his breath until he loses consciousness. Anyone who has ever witnessed this full measure of willful defiance has been shocked by its power. One headstrong three-year-old recently refused to obey a direct command from her mother, saying, "You're just my *mommie,* you know!" Another mere mommie wrote me that she found herself in a similar confrontation with her three-year-old son over something that she wanted him to eat. He was so enraged by her insistence that he refused to eat or drink *anything* for two full days. He became weak and lethargic, but steadfastly held his ground. The mother was worried and guilt ridden, as might be expected. Finally, in desperation, the father looked the child in the eyes and convinced him that he was going to receive a spanking he would never forget if he didn't eat his dinner. With that maneuver, the contest was over. The toddler surrendered. He began to consume everything he could get his hands on, and virtually emptied the refrigerator.

Now tell me, please, why have so few child development authorities recognized this willful defiance? Why have they written so little about it? My guess is that the acknowledgement of childish imperfection would not fit neatly with the humanistic notion that little people are infused with sunshine and goodness, and merely "learn" the meaning of evil. To those who hold that rosy view I can only say, "Take another look!"

The will is not delicate and wobbly. Even for a child in whom the spirit has been sandbagged, there is often a will of steel, making him a threat to himself and others as well.

Such a person can sit on a bridge threatening to jump, while the entire army, navy, and local fire department try to save his life. My point is that the will is malleable. It can and should be molded and polished—not to make a robot of a child for our selfish purposes, but to give him the ability to control his *own* impulses and exercise self-discipline later in life. In fact, we have a God-given responsibility as parents to shape the will in the manner described in the previous chapter.

On the other hand (and let me give this paragraph the strongest possible emphasis), the *spirit* of a child is a million times more vulnerable than his will. It is a delicate flower that can be crushed and broken all too easily (and even unintentionally). The spirit, as I have defined it, relates to the self-esteem or the personal worth that a child feels. It is *the* most fragile characteristic in human nature, being particularly vulnerable to rejection and ridicule and failure.

How, then, are we to shape the will while preserving the spirit intact? It is accomplished by establishing reasonable boundaries and enforcing them with love, but by avoiding any implication that the child is unwanted, unnecessary, foolish, ugly, dumb, a burden, an embarrassment, or a disastrous mistake. Any accusation that assaults the worth of a child in this way can be costly, such as "You are so stupid!" Or, "Why can't you make decent grades in school like your sister?" Or, "You have been a pain in the neck ever since the day you were born!"

The following letter was sent to me by a mother of three children and illustrates the precise opposite of the principles I am describing. I believe it will be useful to examine this woman's frustrations and the probable causes for her inability to control her defiant son, Billy. (Note: the details of this letter have been changed slightly to conceal the identity of the writer.)

Dear Dr. Dobson:

More than anything else in this world, I want to have a happy family. We have two girls, ages three and five, and a boy who is ten. They don't get along at all. The boy and his father don't get along either. And I find myself screaming at the kids and sitting on my son to keep him from hitting and kicking his sisters.

His teacher of the past year thought he needed to learn better ways of getting along with his classmates. He had some problems on the playground and had a horrible time on the school bus. And he didn't seem to be able to walk from the bus stop to our house without getting in a fight or throwing rocks at somebody. So I usually pick him up and bring him home myself.

He is very bright but writes poorly and hates to do it. He is impulsive and quick tempered (we all are now). He is tall and strong. Our pediatrician says he has "everything going for him." But Billy seldom finds anything constructive to do. He likes to watch television, play in the water and dig in the dirt.

We are very upset about his diet, but haven't been able to do anything about it. He drinks milk and eats jello and crackers and toast. In the past he ate lots of hot dogs and bologna, but not much lately. He also craves chocolate and bubble gum. We have a grandma nearby who sees that he gets lots of it. She also feeds him baby food. We haven't been able to do anything about that, either.

Billy's teachers, the neighbor children and his sisters complain about him swearing and name-calling. This is really an unfortunate situation because we're *always* thinking of him in a bad light. But hardly a day goes by when something isn't upset or broken. He's been breaking windows since he was a toddler. One day in June he came home early from school and found the house locked, so he threw a rock through his bedroom window, broke it, and crawled in. Another day recently he tried the glass cutter on our bedroom mirror. He spends a great deal of time at the grandma's who caters to him. We feel she is a bad influence, but so are we when we're constantly upset and screaming.

Anyhow, we have what seems to be a hopeless situation. He is growing bigger and stronger but not any wiser. So what do we do or where do we go?

My husband says he refuses to take Billy anywhere ever again until he matures and "acts like a civilized human being." He has threatened to put him in a foster home. I couldn't send him to a foster home. He needs people who know what to do with him. Please help us if you can.

Yours truly,

Mrs. T.

P.S. Our children are adopted and there isn't much of anything left in our marriage.

This is a very sad plea for help, because the writer is undoubtedly sincere in professing "more than anything else in the world I want to have a happy family." From the tone of her letter, however, it is unlikely that she will *ever* realize her greatest desire. In fact, that specific need for peaceful coexistence and harmony has probably led to many of her problems with Billy. The mother is making two very serious mistakes with her son which are among the most common disciplinary errors.

First, Billy's parents have taken no steps to shape his will, although he is begging for their intervention. It is a terrifying thing to be your own boss at ten years of age—unable to find even one adult who is strong enough to earn your respect. Why else would this lad break every rule and attack every figure of authority? Billy waged war on his teacher at school, but she was baffled by his challenge. All she knew to do was to call his trembling mother and report, "Billy needs to learn better ways of getting along with his classmates." (Didn't she phrase it kindly? You can bet there were some stronger things she could have said about his classroom behavior!)

Billy has been an intolerable brat on the school bus, and

he fought with his classmates on the way home, and he broke windows and cut mirrors and used the foulest language and tormented his sisters. He selected the worst possible diet and refused to complete his academic assignments or accept any form of responsibility. Can there be any doubt that Billy was screaming, "Look! I'm doing it all wrong! Doesn't anyone love me enough to care? Can't anyone help me?! I hate the world and the world hates me!"

But Mrs. T's only response to Billy's defiance has been one of utter frustration and distress. She finds herself "screaming at the kids" and "sitting on (her) son" when he misbehaves. Billy is impulsive and quick tempered, but Mrs. T. admits "we all are now." Both she and her husband feel grandma is a bad influence, "but so are we when we are constantly upset and screaming." You see, her only "tool" for control is the use of anger and high-pitched wailing and weeping. There is *no* more ineffective approach to child management than this display of volcanic emotion, as we will see in the following chapter.

Clearly Mrs. T. and her husband have abdicated their responsibilities to provide *leadership* for their family. Note how many times she says, in essence, *we are powerless to act*. These parents were distressed over Billy's poor diet, "but we haven't been able to do anything about it." Billy's grandmother fed him junk food and bubble gum, but "we haven't been able to do anything about that, either." Likewise, they couldn't stop him from swearing or tormenting his sisters or breaking windows or throwing rocks at his peers. We who are observing must wonder, why not? Why is the family ship so difficult to steer? Why is it likely to be dashed to pieces on the rocks or run aground on a sandy beach? The problem is that the ship has no captain! It is drifting aimlessly in the absence of a leader—a decision maker—an authority—who could guide it to safer waters.

Now, please note this second error: instead of shaping Billy's rampaging will, as it desperately needed, *his parents directed their disciplinary efforts at his damaged spirit.* Not only did they scream and cry and wring their hands in despair, but their frustrations gave rise to personal attacks and hostile rejection. Can't you hear his angry father shouting, "Why don't you grow up and act like a civilized human being instead of an intolerable brat?! Well, I'll tell you something! I'm through with you! I'll never take you anywhere again or even let anyone know that you are my son. As a matter of fact, I'm not sure you are going to *be* my son for very long. If you keep acting like a lawless thug we're going to throw you out of this family—we're going to put you in a foster home. Then we'll see how you like it!" And with each accusation, Billy's self-esteem moved down another notch. But did these personal assaults make him sweeter or more cooperative? Of course not! He just became meaner and more bitter and more convinced of his own worthlessness. You see, Billy's spirit had been crushed, but his will raged undiminished at hurricane force. And sadly, he is the kind of individual who, as he grows older, often turns his self-hatred on innocent victims outside his family.

If circumstances permitted, it would be my pleasure to have Billy in our home for a period of time. It's not too late to save him and I would feel challenged by the opportunity to try. How would I approach this defiant youngster? By giving him the following message as soon as his suitcase was unpacked: "Billy, there are several things I want to talk over with you, now that you're a member of our family. First, you'll soon learn how much we love you in this house. I'm glad you're here, and I hope these will be the happiest days of your life. And you should know that I care about your feelings and problems and concerns. We invited you here because we wanted you to come, and you will have the same love and respect our own children receive. If you have something to say to me, you can come right out and say it. I won't get angry or make you regret expressing yourself. Neither my wife nor I will ever intentionally do anything to hurt you or treat you unkindly. You'll see that these are not just empty promises that you're hearing. This is the way people act when they love each other, and we already love you.

"But, Billy, there are some other things you must also understand. There are going to be some definite rules and acceptable ways to behave in this home, and you are going to have to live within these boundaries just as our other children do. You will carry your share of responsibilities and jobs, and your school work will be given high priority each evening. And you need to understand, Billy, that my most important job as your guardian is to see that you behave in ways that are healthy to yourself and others. It may take you a week or two to adjust to this new situation, but you're going to make it and I'm going to be here to help you. And when you refuse to obey, I will punish you immediately. This will help you change some of the harmful, destructive ways you've learned to behave. But even when I must discipline you, I will love you as much as I do right now."

The first time Billy disobeyed what he knew to be my definite instructions, I would react decisively. There would be no screaming or derogatory accusations, although he would soon know that I meant what I had said. He would probably be given a stiff spanking and sent to bed an hour or two early. The following morning we would discuss the issue rationally, reassure him of our continuing love, and then start over. Most delinquent children respond beautifully to this one-two punch of love, and consistent discipline. It's an unbeatable combination!

To repeat, our guiding purpose is to shape the child's will without breaking his spirit. This dual objective is outlined for us throughout the Scriptures, but is specifically stated in two important references:

Shaping the will
> He (the father) must have the proper authority in his own household and be able to control and command the respect of his children. 1 Tim. 3:4, 5 (Phillips)

Preserving the spirit
> And now a word to you parents. Don't keep on scolding and nagging your children, making them angry and resentful. Rather, bring them up with loving discipline the Lord himself approves, with suggestions and godly advice. Ephesians 6:4 (TLB)

QUESTIONS

Question: You probably remember the very popular book of a few years ago, entitled *Jonathan Livingston Seagull*. It was about a gull who refused to cooperate with the flock and follow the dictates of his "society." The real meaning of the book, of course, related to the virtues of individuality and independence in the *human* family. Will you comment on the book and its deeper theme.

Answer: This book expressed a damaging philosophy that became popular about eight years ago, which can be summarized by the phrase "Do your own thing." It means, in brief, that I'm protecting my own self-interests and will do whatever suits my fancy, regardless of the needs of others or the moral values of my society. Other words have been used to express the same selfish orientation, including "Looking out for ol' number one," and "If it feels good, do it." This hedonistic viewpoint inspired many other books and songs, including a heart-wrenching ballad by Sammy Davis, Jr. entitled "I've Gotta Be Me." (Who else could he be, pray tell?) It was also responsible for an incredibly brazen recording by Frank Sinatra, titled "I Did It My Way."

It is my conviction that these messages are directly contradictory to the essence of Christianity which puts its emphasis on giving, sharing, caring, loving, turning the other cheek, going the second mile, and accepting God's commandments. Furthermore, extreme selfishness has the power to blow a family (or a society) off the face of the earth. I wonder how many mothers and fathers of that era took flight, as suggested by J. L. Seagull, in search of an individuality at any price? Waiting at home were vulnerable kids who will carry the scars of parental rejection until the day they die! It has been my sad responsibility to treat some of these little victims whose parents were proudly "doing it their way."

Philip Yancey wrote the following statement about sea gulls as related to human behavior:

> It's easy to see why people like the sea gull. I've sat overlooking a craggy harbor and watched one. He exults in freedom. He thrusts his wings backward with powerful strokes, climbing higher, higher until he's above all other gulls, then coasts downward in majestic loops and circles. He constantly performs, as if he knows a movie camera is trained on him, recording.
>
> In a flock, though, the sea gull is a different bird.

His majesty and dignity melt into a sordid slough of in-fighting and cruelty. Watch that same gull as he dive-bombs into a group of gulls, provoking a flurry of scattered feathers and angry squawks, to steal a tiny morsel of meat. The concepts of sharing and manners do not exist among gulls. They are so fiercely competitive and jealous that if you tie a red ribbon around the leg of one gull, making him stand out, you sentence him to execution. The others in his flock will furiously attack him with claws and beaks, hammering through feathers and flesh to draw blood. They'll continue until he lies flattened in a bloody heap.[2]

If we must select a bird to serve as a model for our society the sea gull is not the best choice. Yancey has suggested that we consider the behavior of geese, instead. Have you ever wondered why these remarkable birds fly in "V" formation? Science has recently learned that the flock actually travels up to 71 percent faster and easier by maintaining this pattern. The goose on the point of the "V" has the most difficult assignment, resulting from greater wind resistance. Thus, that lead position is rotated every few minutes in the air, which permits the flock to fly long distances without rest. The easiest flight is experienced at the two rear sections of the formation and, remarkably, the strong geese permit the young, weak, and old birds to occupy those less strenuous positions. It is even believed that the constant "honking" of the flock is a method by which the stronger birds encourage the laggards. Furthermore, if a goose becomes too tired or is ill and has to drop out of the flock, he is never abandoned. A healthy bird will follow the ailing one to the ground and wait with him until he can continue in flight. This cooperation within the social order contributes greatly to the survival and well-being of the flock.

Yancey concludes,

> The sea gull teaches me to break loose and fly. But the goose goes farther: he teaches me to fly "in a family." With the support of friends and Christians who care for me, I can far outstrip the aeronautical feats of any sea gulls. I can fly further with the family than I ever could alone. And as I fly, my effort helps each other member of the family.

Alas, there are times when I feel our society consists of 200 million solitary sea gulls, each huffing and puffing to do his own thing, but paying an enormous price in loneliness and stress for his individuality.

Question: Why do children seem to love teachers who are the strongest disciplinarians?

Answer: Well, your statement is only partially true. No one likes a mean old grouch, even if he does maintain strict order and deportment. But you are right in implying that children are drawn to the teacher who can control a class without sacrificing an attitude of love and pleasantness. And that is a highly developed art which most topnotch teachers have discovered.

In answer to your question, children love good disciplinarians primarily because they are afraid of each other and want the security of a leader who can provide a safe atmosphere. *Anything* can happen in the absence of adult leadership.

NOTE: I have deliberately deleted references to classroom discipline in this book. A subsequent book is planned on the subject of discipline for teachers.

Question: Do you think some children are unintentionally cruel to each other?

Answer: I am certain of it. In fact, I lived it. When I was approximately eight years old, I attended a Sunday school class as a regular member. One morning a visitor entered our class and sat down. His name was Fred, and I can still see his face. More important, I can still see Fred's ears. They were curved in the shape of a reversed "C," and protruded noticeably. I was fascinated by the shape of Fred's unusual ears because they reminded me of jeep fenders (we were deep into World War II at the time). Without thinking of Fred's feelings, I pointed out his strange feature to my friends, who all thought Jeep Fenders was a terribly funny name for a boy with bent ears. Fred seemed to think it was funny, too, and he chuckled along with the rest of us. Suddenly, Fred stopped laughing. He jumped to his feet, red in the face (and ears), and rushed to the door crying. He bolted into the hall and ran from the building. Fred never returned to our class.

I remember my shock over Fred's violent and unexpected reaction. You see, I had *no* idea that I was embarrassing him by my little joke. I was a sensitive kid and often defended the underdog, even when I was a youngster. I would *never* have hurt a visitor on purpose—and that is precisely my point. Looking back on the episode, I hold my teachers and my parents responsible for that event. They should have told me what it feels like to be laughed at . . . especially for something different about your body. My mother, who was very wise with children, has since admitted that she should have taught me to feel for others. And as for the Sunday school leaders, I don't remember what their curriculum consisted of at that time, but what better content could they have presented than the *real* meaning of the commandment, "Love thy neighbor as thyself"?

Question: I know that adoption is common today, and children should be able to take the news in stride. But I'm still uneasy about explaining this matter to my toddler and would like some advice on "how to."

Answer: The best answer I've found for that question was written by Dr. Milton I. Levine, as published in *Your Child from 2 to 5*.[3] I'll quote his statement and then comment on his views:

Common-Sense Approaches to Adoption

ADOPTING children has become such an accepted practice these days that the quavering question, *"Shall I tell him he's adopted?"* doesn't even qualify as soap-opera dialogue any more. Most parents realize that telling a youngster from the earliest possible moment provides the only solid foundation for his and their security.

However, as Dr. Milton I. Levine, advisory board member of *2-to-5 World News* and Associate Professor of Pediatrics, New York Hospital–Cornell Medical Center, points out: "Even though adoption is no longer regarded as a shameful secret but rightly as a logical matter of fact, the situation still demands delicacy, understanding, and many common-sense decisions on the part of parents."

Parents should tell the child about his adoption from the time he begins to beg for stories, says Dr. Levine. This will spare the youngster serious shock that can accompany the revelation in later years. Parents might treat the story as a wondrous chapter in the family's history. But the tendency to put off a decision sometimes affects even the best-intentioned adoptive parents. "Let's wait until he's old enough to understand," they may say, and delay the explanation until a basic fact turns into a dark secret. In Dr. Levine's opinion, even five- and six-year-olds are too old to be told without resultant emotional damage. He urges parents to:

1. Tell the child about his adoption from the moment he is ready to listen to stories.
2. Use the word "adopted" in the narrative until it becomes a synonym for "chosen" and "selected" and "wanted."
3. Make no attempt to conceal the adoption, even though moving into a new neighborhood might invite concealment.

"Some adoptive parents never seem to outgrow an apologetic attitude based on a feeling that they are merely pinch-hitting for the child's 'own' parents," says Dr. Levine. "For their own mental health, as well as their child's, they must accept the fact that they are, in reality, the youngster's parents. The mother and father who raise a child from infancy, giving him the love and care that enable him to grow freely, *are* the *real* parents; the strangers who produced the baby are merely *biological* parents. The difference can't be stressed strongly enough. By imparting to the child, even unconsciously, an unjustified feeling of loss—a feeling that he *had parents*, but now has substitutes, however loving—these adoptive parents endanger the child's security in his closest relationships and retard his understanding of the true role of parent."

Even professionals are divided over what to tell adopted children about their biological parents, Dr. Levine admits. There are at least three possible approaches, he points out, but not one can qualify as an answer:

1. Tell the child his biological parents are dead.
2. State plainly that the biological parents were unable to care for their baby themselves.
3. Tell the child nothing is known about the biological parents, but that he was secured from an agency dedicated to finding good homes for babies.

"There are pros and cons to all of these solutions," emphasizes Dr. Levine, who prefers the first approach because: "The child who is told that his biological parents are dead is free to love the mother and father he lives with. He won't be tormented by a haunting obligation to search for his biological parents when he's grown.

"Since the possibility of losing one's parents is one of childhood's greatest fears, it is true that the youngster who is told that his biological parents are dead may feel that all parents —including his second set—are pretty impermanent," concedes Dr. Levine. "Nevertheless, I feel that in the long run the child will find it easier to adjust to death than to abandonment. To tell a youngster that his parents gave him up because they were unable to take care of him is to present him with a complete rejection. He cannot comprehend the circumstances which might lead to such an act. But an unwholesome view of himself as an unwanted object, not worth fighting to keep, might be established."

Sex education is another thorny problem for adoptive parents. Any simple, natural explanation of reproduction stresses that a baby is conceived out of his mother's and father's love for each other and their desire to have a child. This explanation is reassuring to other children. But it may, because of the complexity of his situation, cause the adopted child to feel estranged from his adoptive parents, dubious about his own beginnings, and a little out of step with nature in general.

I would disagree with Dr. Levine only in reference to comments made about the biological parents. I am unwilling to lie to my child about anything, and would not tell him that his natural parents were dead if that were not true. Sooner or later, he will learn that he has been misled, which could bring the entire adoption story under suspicion.

Instead, I would be inclined to tell the child that very little is known about his biological parents. Several inoffensive and vague possibilities could be offered to him, such as, "We can only guess at the reasons the man and woman could not take care of a baby. They may have been extremely poor and unable to give you the care you needed; or perhaps the woman was sick; or she may not have had a home. We just don't know. But we *do* know that we're thankful that you could come be our son (or daughter), which was one of the greatest gifts God ever gave to us."

Furthermore, I would add three suggestions to Dr. Levine's comments. First, Christian parents should present the adoptive event as a tremendous blessing (as implied above) that brought great excitement to the household. Tell about praying for a child and waiting impatiently for God's answer. Then describe how the news came that the Lord had answered those prayers, and how the whole family thanked Him for His gift of love. Let your child know your delight when you first saw him lying in a crib, and how cute he looked in his blue blanket, etc. Tell him that his adoption was one of the happiest days of your life, and how you raced to the telephone to call all your friends and family members to share the fantastic news. (Again, I'm assuming that these details are true.) Tell him the story of Moses' adoption by Pharaoh's daughter, and how God chose him for a great work with the children of Israel. Look for other, similar illustrations which convey respect and dignity to the adoptee. You see the child's interpretation of the adoptive event is almost totally dependent on the manner in which it is conveyed during the early years. Most certainly, one does not want to approach the subject sadly, admitting reluctantly that a dark and troublesome secret must now be confessed.

Second, celebrate *two* birthdays with equal gusto each year: the anniversary of his birth, and the anniversary of the day he became your son (or daughter). While other natural children in the family celebrate one birthday, the second hoopla will give the adopted child a compensative edge to offset any differences he might feel relative to his siblings. And use the word "adopted" openly and freely, until it loses its esoteric sting.

Third, when the foundation has been laid and the issue defused, then forget it. Don't constantly remind the child of his uniqueness to the point of foolishness. Mention the matter when it is appropriate, but don't reveal anxiety or tension by constantly throwing adoption in the child's face. Youngsters are amazingly perceptive at "reading" these thinly disguised attitudes.

I believe it is possible, by following these common sense suggestions, to raise an adopted child without psychological trauma or personal insult.

4 The Common Errors

Dr. Benjamin Spock, noted pediatrician and author, has been severely criticized in recent years for his laissez-faire approach to child rearing. He has been blamed for weakening parental authority and producing an entire generation of disrespectful and unruly children. To the man on the street, Dr. Spock has become a symbol of permissiveness and overindulgence in parent-child relationships.

Despite his wishy-washy reputation, Dr. Spock published an article several years ago in *Redbook* Magazine which was clearly supportive of firm discipline. Consider the fol-

lowing quotations from that surprising publication entitled,
"How Not to Bring Up a Bratty Child":[1]

> Inability to be firm is, to my mind, the commonest problem
> of parents in America today.
>
> A parent says, "Lunch is ready—come in now." The child
> pretends not to hear and the parent, despite her realization
> that the child is not going to cooperate on occasions such
> as this, dodges the issue and goes indoors.
>
> A parent says, "It's cold today; you should wear your
> snowsuit." The eight-year-old child says, "I don't want to,"
> and the parent doesn't reply. Fifteen minutes later the same
> conversation is repeated and comes to the same inconclusive
> ending.
>
> A child says, "I want another piece of candy." The parent
> says, "You know you are meant to have only one." The child
> says, "But I want another," and slowly takes it, watching
> to be sure that the parent doesn't get angry. The parent de-
> cides to let it pass.
>
> None of these episodes are at all serious in themselves. If
> they continue, however, the child's personality will become
> balkier and peskier as the months and years go by. The wear
> and tear on the parents from this kind of low-key battling
> is painful and exhausting.
>
> The commonest reason, I think, why parents can't be firm
> is that they're afraid that if they insist, their children will
> resent them or at least won't love them as much. You can
> see this clearly in an extreme case in which a bratty child can
> get what she or he wants by shouting, "I hate you!" The
> parent looks dismayed and gives in promptly.
>
> Of course most of us dislike unpleasantness, and prefer
> for this reason to accommodate others, including our own
> children. But that's not a sensible reason for giving in to
> them unreasonably, since we sense that this only invites more
> demands and arguments.

And in conclusion, Dr. Spock wrote:

> The way to get a child to do what must be done or stop
> doing what shouldn't be done is to be clear and definite each
> time. Part of the definiteness consists of keeping an eye on
> her until she complies. I'm not recommending the overbear-

ing manner of a drill sergeant that would rub anyone the wrong way. The manner can be and should be friendly. A firm, calm approach makes the child much more likely to cooperate—politely, promptly and completely.

I know this is true. I've seen it work not just hundreds but thousands of times. Parental firmness also makes for a happier child.

I found the content of this article to be refreshing and yet confusing. Could these traditional views have been written by Dr. Benjamin Spock—the great paragon of permissiveness? Could the world's most famous anti-disciplinarian actually be recommending parental firmness and authority? I finally concluded that the aging pediatrician must have reevaluated his views and revised some of his earlier recommendations and conclusions.

I was impressed by the courage that was required for Dr. Spock to write such an article. Perhaps the most difficult assignment for any lofty professional is to state publicly, in effect, "I was wrong." It would be even more difficult for the pediatrician to admit his errors, considering the criticism he has received during the past decade. Nevertheless, he confessed in the *Redbook* publication, "We didn't realize, until it was too late, how our know-it-all attitude was undermining the self assurance of parents."[2]

I appreciated his candor and felt compelled to send him a cordial letter to convey my respect. I thanked him for the courage he demonstrated and complimented his views which correlated so well with my own. Then I stated,

In actuality, neither of us formulated those principles which you expressed so eloquently this month. They were inspired by the Creator of children more than 2000 years ago. Isn't it interesting that He is always right in the final analysis?

Included with my letter to Dr. Spock was a copy of my book *Dare to Discipline*. (That took some gall.) Several weeks later, I received the following reply from his office in New York.

BENJAMIN   SPOCK,   M.   D.
SECRETARIAL ADDRESS (THIRD FLOOR)
538 MADISON AVENUE
NEW YORK, NEW YORK 10022

SECRETARIAL PHONE
(212) 421-1085

April 13, 1974

James Dobson, Ph.D.
Childrens Hospital of Los Angeles
4650 Sunset Boulevard
P.O. Box 54700
Los Angeles, California 90054

Dear Dr. Dobson:

Thank you for your book and your letter.

Actually my February article contains nothing that
I haven't said again and again for 25 years. It was
those who hadn't read BABY AND CHILD CARE and my magazine
articles but who resented my opposition to the war in
Vietnam who called my a permissivist.

Sincerely,

Benjamin Spock

Whereas I had been unable to harmonize the *Redbook* views with Dr. Spock's reputation, I was even more confused by the content of his letter. His article was definitely self-critical and apologetic in tone, yet he claimed to have said nothing new or unique in that statement. The puzzle appeared to be indecipherable.

Later in 1974, I was granted an opportunity to meet Dr. Spock in person. We were both guests on Barbara Walters' "Not for Women Only" television show, along with two other panel members who write for parents, Dr. Helen

Derosis and Dr. Lee Salk. We taped five programs that one day, although the shows were broadcast throughout an entire week. (After a program has been filmed, the hostess and guests retire backstage for a few minutes, change coats and ties or dresses, and return to the set. Thus it appears that five different visits have been made to the studio, when in reality the programs are shot back-to-back.)

I was seated beside Dr. Spock throughout the five-part series, and we ate lunch together. Therefore, I had approximately six hours to get acquainted with the physician whose first book for parents sold 28 million copies and has been published in dozens of languages. We talked about his views on child rearing, and ultimately discussed his article in *Redbook* Magazine.

Based on these conversations, I am firmly convinced that Dr. Benjamin Spock believes in the value of consistent discipline and parental leadership. His reputation for permissiveness is largely unjustified, and is, in fact, a matter that he resents deeply. Dr. Spock blames Dr. Norman Vincent Peale for confusing the public on his views, and believes that the minister's deeper motive was to discredit him for his passivist stance on the Viet Nam war. I can't speak for Dr. Peale, but I do believe Dr. Spock's views have been grossly misrepresented to the American public. I found him to be a very gentle, unassuming man who did not seek the parental influence that fell to him. He told me he agreed to write *Baby and Child Care* only because the publisher assured him that it could be done quickly and "didn't have to be a great book."

It is obvious that Dr. Spock and I are in opposite camps on many issues; he is a political liberal and I tend to be conservative. He is a Freudian and I am most certainly not. He apparently does not share my Christian perspective. However, on the issue of discipline, I do not find myself in disagreement with the views he now expresses. Toward the end of the final "Not for Women Only" program, actress Polly Bergen (filling in for Barbara Walters) asked the panel members, one by one, if we believed in spankings. All four of us endorsed the use of corporal punishment when appropriate, including Dr. Benjamin Spock. And if his earlier writings are examined carefully, one can find the recommendations for parental control represented, but not emphasized, therein. Very little was written which would earn him the title of "Ultimate Permissivist," although he recommended following permissive feeding schedules. (I certainly agree that babies should be fed when they are hungry, regardless of the clock or some arbitrary feeding plan.) Throughout his book, I feel he took a rather reasonable approach to parent-child relationships.

Why have I gone to considerable lengths to set the record straight with regard to Dr. Spock's views? Perhaps I feel I owe the man an apology for having contributed to the confusion in my earlier statements about his work. But also, the American people who are angry over the present permissive trends in this country should know that they are shooting at the wrong target. There are thousands of psychologists, psychiatrists, and self-appointed experts around us who are offering far more foolish recommendations than does the aging pediatrician. One of those writers, educator John Holt, is quoted in a subsequent chapter and makes Dr. Spock appear downright oppressive by comparison.

Another reason for referring to Dr. Spock's article in *Redbook* Magazine is to emphasize one of his observations which I have also found to be extremely important. He stated,

> A child—let's say a girl—instantly detects parental hesitancy, parental guilt, parental crossness. These

attitudes challenge her to resist requests and to demand more privileges. Her peskiness in turn makes the parent increasingly resentful inside, until this finally explodes in a display of anger—great or small —that convinces the child she must give in. In other words, parental submissiveness doesn't avoid unpleasantness; it makes it inevitable.[3]

How accurate is this statement by Dr. Spock! The parent who is most anxious to avoid conflict and confrontation often finds himself screaming and threatening and ultimately thrashing the child. Indeed, child abuse may be the end result.

This leads us to *the* most common error in disciplining children, and perhaps the most costly. I am referring to the inappropriate use of *anger* in attempting to control boys or girls. I touched this subject in *Dare to Discipline*, but I feel it must be given greater stress at this point.

There is no more ineffective method of controlling human beings (of all ages) than the use of irritation and anger. Nevertheless, *most* adults rely primarily on their own emotional response to secure the cooperation of children. One teacher said on a national television program, "I like being a professional educator, but I hate the daily task of teaching. My children are so unruly that I have to stay mad at them all the time just to control the classroom." How utterly frustrating to be required to be mean and angry as part of a routine assignment, year in and year out. Yet many teachers (and parents) know of no other way to lead children. Believe me, it is exhausting and it doesn't work!

Consider your *own* motivational system. Suppose you are driving your automobile home from work this evening, and you exceed the speed limit by forty miles per hour.

Standing on the street corner is a lone policeman who has not been given the means to arrest you. He has no squad car or motorcycle; he wears no badge, carries no gun, and can write no tickets. All he is commissioned to do is stand on the curb and scream insults as you speed past. Would you slow down just because he shakes his fist in protest? Of course not! You might wave to him as you streak by. His anger would achieve little except to make him appear comical and foolish.

On the other hand, nothing influences the way Mr. Motorist drives more than occasionally seeing a black and white vehicle in hot pursuit with nineteen red lights flashing in the rear view mirror. When his car is brought to a stop, a dignified, courteous patrolman approaches the driver's window. He is six foot nine, has a voice like the Lone Ranger, and carries a sawed-off shotgun on each hip. "Sir," he says firmly but politely, "our radar unit indicates you were traveling sixty-five miles per hour in a twenty-five-mile zone. May I see your driver's license, please?" He opens his leatherbound book of citations and leans toward you. He has revealed no hostility and offers no criticisms, yet you immediately go to pieces. You fumble nervously to locate the small document in your wallet (the one with the horrible Polaroid picture). Why are your hands moist and your mouth dry? Why is your heart thumping in your throat? Because the course of *action* that John Law is about to take is notoriously unpleasant. Alas, it is his *action* which dramatically affects your future driving habits.

Disciplinary action influences behavior; anger does not. As a matter of fact, I am convinced that adult anger produces a destructive kind of disrespect in the minds of our children. They perceive that our frustration is caused by our inability to control the situation. We represent justice to them, yet we're on the verge of tears as we flail the air with our hands and shout empty threats and warnings. Let me ask: Would *you* respect a superior court judge who behaved that emotionally in administering legal justice? Certainly not. This is why the judicial system is carefully controlled to appear objective, rational, and dignified.

I am not recommending that parents and teachers conceal their legitimate emotions from their children. I am not suggesting that we be like bland and unresponsive robots who hold everything inside. There are times when our boys and girls become insulting or disobedient and our irritation is entirely appropriate. In fact, it *should* be revealed, or else we appear phony and unreal. My point is merely that anger often becomes a *tool* used consciously for the purpose of influencing behavior. It is ineffective and can be damaging to the relationship between generations.

Let's look at a specific illustration that could represent any one of twenty million homes this afternoon. Henry is in the second grade and arrives home from school in a whirlwind of activity. He has been wiggling and giggling since he awakened this morning, but incredibly, he still has excess energy to burn. His mother, Mrs. Gerritol, is not in the same condition. She has been on her feet since staggering out of bed at 6:30 A.M. She fixed breakfast for the family, cleaned the mess, got Dad off to work, and sent Henry to school, and then settled into a long day trying to keep her twin toddlers from killing themselves. By the time Henry blows in from school, she has put in eight hours' work without a rest. (Toddlers don't take breaks, so why should their mothers?)

Despite Mom's fatigue, she can hardly call it a day. She still has at least six hours of work left to do, including going to the grocery store, fixing the evening meal, washing the dishes, giving the twins their baths, putting on their diapers, tucking them in bed, helping Henry with his homework, joining in his prayers, brushing his teeth, reading him a story, saying good-night, and then bringing him four glasses of water throughout the closing forty-five minutes of the evening. I get depressed just thinking about the weary Mrs. Gerritol and her domestic duties.

Henry is not so sympathetic, however, and arrives home from school in a decidedly mischievous mood. He can't find anything interesting to do, so he begins to irritate his uptight mother. He teases one of the twins to the point of tears, and pulls the cat's tail, and spills the dog's water. Mother is nagging by this time, but Henry acts like he doesn't hear her. Then he goes to the toy closet and begins jerking out games and boxes of plastic toys and Pickup Stix. Mom knows that someone is going to have to clean up all that mess and she has a vague notion about who will get the assignment. The intensity of her voice is rising again. She orders him to the bathroom to wash his hands in preparation for dinner. Henry is gone for fifteen minutes, and when he returns his hands are still dirty. Mom's pulse is pounding through her veins by this time, and there is a definite migraine sensation above her left eye.

Finally, the day wears down to its concluding responsibility: Henry's bedtime. But Henry does not *want* to go to bed and he knows it will take his harassed mother at least thirty minutes to get him there. Henry does not do *anything* against his wishes unless his mother becomes very angry and "blows up" at him. Mrs. Gerritol begins the emotional process of coercing her reluctant son to take his bath and prepare for bed. This portion of the story was included in *Dare to Discipline,* and we will quote from that description:[4]

Eight-year-old Henry is sitting on the floor, playing with his games. Mom looks at her watch and says, "Henry, it's nearly nine o'clock (a thirty minute exaggeration) so gather up your junk and go take your bath." Now Henry knows, and Mom knows, that she doesn't mean for him to go take a bath. She merely meant for him to start *thinking* about going to take his bath. She would have fainted dead away if he had responded to her empty command. Approximately ten minutes later, Mom speaks again, "Now, Henry, it is getting later and you have to go to school tomorrow, and I want those toys picked up; then go get in that tub!" She still does not intend for Henry to obey, and he knows it. Her *real* message is "We're getting closer, Hank." Henry shuffles around and stacks a box or two to demonstrate that he heard her. Then he settles down for a few more minutes of play. Six minutes pass, and Mom issues another command, this time with more passion and threat in her voice. "Now listen, young man, I told you to get a move on, and I meant it." To Henry, this means he must get his toys picked up and meander toward the bathroom door. If his mom pursues him with a rapid step, then he must carry out the assignment posthaste. However, if Mom's mind wanders before she performs the last step of this ritual, Henry is free to enjoy a few more seconds reprieve.

You see, Henry and his mom are involved in a one-act play; they both know the rules and the role being enacted by the opposite player. The entire scene is programmed, computerized, and scripted. Whenever Mom wants Henry to do something he dislikes, she progresses through graduated steps of phony anger, beginning with calm and ending with a red flush and a threat. Henry does not have to move until she reaches the peak anger point. How foolish this game is! Since Mom controls him by the use of empty threats she has to stay mad all the time. Her relationship with her children is contaminated, and she ends each day with a pounding, throbbing headache. She can never count on instant obedience; it takes her at least 20 minutes to work up a believable degree of anger.

How much better it is to use *action* to get action. There are hundreds of tools which will bring the desired response, some of which involve pain while others offer the child a reward. . . . Minor pain can provide excellent motivation for the child, when appropriate. You see, the parent should have some means of making the child want to cooperate, other than simply obeying because he was told to do so. For those who can think of no such device, I will suggest one: there is a muscle, lying snugly against the base of the neck. Anatomy books list it as the trapezius muscle, and when firmly squeezed, it sends little messengers to the brain saying, "This hurts; avoid recurrence at all costs." The pain is only temporary; it can cause no damage. When the youngster ignores being told to do something by his parent, he should know that Mom has a practical recourse.

Let's return to the bedtime issue between Henry and his Mom; she should have told him that he had fifteen more minutes to play. It then would have been wise to set the alarm clock or the stove buzzer to sound in fifteen minutes. No one, child or adult, likes a sudden interruption to his activity. When the time came, Mom should have quietly told Henry to go take his bath. If he didn't move immediately, the shoulder muscle could have been squeezed. If Henry learns that this procedure is invariably followed, he will move before the consequence is applied.

There will be those among my readers who feel that the deliberate, premeditated application of minor pain to a sweet little child is a harsh and unloving recommendation. I ask those skeptics to hear me out. Consider the alternatives. On the one hand, there is constant nagging and strife between parent and child. When the youngster discovers there is no threat behind the millions of words he hears, he stops listening to them. The only messages he responds to are those reaching a peak of emotion, which means there is much screaming and yelling going on. The child is pulling in the opposite direction, fraying Mom's nerves and straining the parent-child relationship. But the most important limitation of these verbal reprimands is that their user often has to resort to physical punishment in the end, anyway. Thus, instead of the discipline being administered in a calm and judicious manner, the parent has become unnerved and frustrated, swinging wildly at the belligerent child. There was no reason for a fight to have occurred. The situation could have ended very differently if the parental attitude had been one of confident serenity. Speaking softly, almost pleasantly, Mom says, "Henry, you know what happens when you don't mind me; now I don't see any reason in the world why I should have to make you feel pain to get your cooperation tonight, but if you insist, I'll play the game with you. When the buzzer sounds you let me know what your decision is." The child has a choice to make, and the advantages to him of obeying his mother's wishes are clear. She need not scream. She need not threaten to shorten his life. She need not become upset. She is in command. Of course, Mother will have to prove two or three times that she will apply the pain, if necessary, and occasionally throughout the coming months her child will check to see if she is still at the helm. But there is no question in my mind as to which of these two approaches involves the least pain and the least hostility between parent and child.

An understanding of the interaction between Henry and his mother can be very helpful to parents who have become

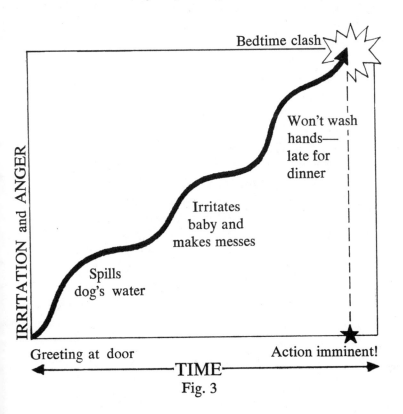

Fig. 3

"screamers" and don't know why. Let's look at their relationship during that difficult evening as diagrammed on
Figure 3. Note that Henry's mother greeted him at the
front door after school, which represented a low point of
irritation. From that time forward, however, her emotion
built and intensified until it reached a moment of explosion
at the end of the day.

By her ultimate display of anger at bedtime, Mrs. Gerritol made it clear to Henry that she was through warning
and was now ready to take definite action. You see, most
parents (even those who are very permissive) have a point
on the scale beyond which they will not be pushed; inevitable punishment looms immediately across that line. The
amazing thing about children is that they know *precisely*
where their parents typically draw the line. We adults reveal our particular points of action to them in at least a
dozen subtle ways: only at those moments do we use their
middle names (William Thornton Langford, get in the
tub!!). Our speech also becomes more staccato and abrupt,
(Young! Man! I! Told! You! . . . .) Our faces turn red
(an important clue), we jump from our chairs, and Junior
knows it is time to cooperate.

The other interesting thing about children is that having
identified the circumstances which immediately precede
disciplinary action, they will take their parents directly to
that barrier and bump it repeatedly, but will *seldom* go beyond it deliberately. Once or twice Henry will ignore his
mother's emotional fireworks, just to see if she has the courage to deliver on her promise. When that question has been
answered, he will do what she demands in the nick of time
to avoid punishment.

Now this brings us to the punch line for this important
discussion. I must admit that what I am about to write is
difficult to express and may not be fully understood by my

readers. It can, however, be of value to parents who want to stop fighting with their children.

I have said that parental anger often signals to Junior that he has reached his action line. Therefore, he obeys, albeit reluctantly, only when Mom or Dad "get mad," indicating that they will now resort to punishment. On the other hand, the parents observe that Junior's surrender occurs simultaneously with their anger and inaccurately conclude that their emotional explosion is what forced him to yield. Thus, their anger seems necessary for control in the future. They have grossly misunderstood the situation.

Returning to the story of Henry, his mother told him six or eight times to take his bath. Only when she "blew up" did he get in the tub, leading her to believe that her anger produced his obedience. She is wrong! It was not her anger that sent Hank to the suds—it was the *action* which he believed to be imminent. Her anger was nothing more than a tip-off that Mom was frustrated enough to spank his pink bottom. Henry *cares* about that!

I have written this entire chapter in order to convey this one message: you don't *need* anger to control children. You *do* need action, occasionally. Furthermore, you can apply the action anywhere on the time line that is convenient, and children will live contentedly within that boundary. In fact, the closer the action moves to the front of the conflict the less punishment is required. A pinch of the trapezius muscle would not be a sufficient deterrent at the end of a two-hour struggle, whereas it is more than adequate when the conflict is minimal. (Incidentally, I do not recommend that mothers weighing less than ninety pounds try to squeeze the shoulder muscles of their big teen-agers. There are definite risks involved in that procedure. The general rule to follow is, "If you can't reach it, don't squeeze it.")

Let me return to Dr. Spock's valuable observation, particularly as it applies to the diagram. "Parental submissive-ness (by that he refers to parents who have *no action line,* or else it occurs too late) doesn't avoid unpleasantness; it makes it inevitable." (If you don't take a stand early, a child is *compelled* by his nature to push you further.) The child's defiance, then, "makes the parent increasingly more resentful, until it finally explodes in a display of anger." That is precisely what I have been attempting to say for the past thirteen years!

Contained in this statement is an understanding of children which some adults grasp intuitively, while others never quite "feel it." It involves the delicate balance between love and control, recognizing that a reasonable and consistent action-line does not assault self-worth, but represents a source of security for an immature child.

Fathers often comprehend this principle better than mothers, for reasons which escape me. Thus, it is very common for a mother to say to me: "I don't understand my kids. They will do exactly what their father demands, but they won't mind me at all." The behavior of her children is no mystery. They are bright enough to notice that Dad draws his action line earlier than Mother. She screams and argues, while he quietly acts.

Children often understand these forces even better than their parents who are bogged down with adult responsibilities and worries. That is why so many kids are able to win the contest of wills; they devote their *primary* effort to the game, while we grownups play only when we must. One father overheard his five-year-old daughter, Laura, say to her little sister who was doing something wrong, "Mmmmm, I'm going to tell Mommie on you. No! I'll tell Daddy. He's worse!" Laura had evaluated the disciplinary measures of her two parents, and concluded that one was more effective than the other.

This same child was observed by her father to have become especially disobedient and defiant. She was irritating other family members and looking for ways to avoid minding her parents. Her dad decided not to confront her directly about this change in behavior, but to punish her consistently for every offense until she settled down. Thus, for three or four days, he let Laura get away with nothing. She was spanked, stood in the corner, and sent to her bedroom. At the conclusion of the fourth day, she was sitting on the bed with her father and younger sister. Without provocation, Laura pulled the hair of the toddler who was looking at a book. Her dad promptly thumped her on the head with his large hand. Laura did not cry, but sat in silence for a moment or two, and then said, "Hurrummph! All my tricks are not working!"

If the reader will recall his own childhood years, he will probably remember similar events in which the disciplinary techniques of adults were analyzed consciously and their weaknesses probed. When I was a child, I once spent the night with a rambunctious friend who seemed to know every move his parents were going to make. Earl was like a military general who had deciphered the enemy code, permitting him to outmaneuver his opponents at every turn. After we were tucked into our own twin beds that night, he gave me an astounding description of his father's temper.

Earl said, "When my dad gets very angry, he uses some really bad words that will amaze you." (He listed three or four startling examples from past experience.)

I replied, "I don't believe it!"

Mr. Walker was a very tall, reserved man who seemed to have it all together. I just couldn't conceive of his saying the words Earl had quoted.

"Want me to prove it to you?" said Earl mischievously. "All we have to do is keep on laughing and talking instead of going to sleep. My dad will come and tell us to be quiet over and over, and he'll get madder and madder every time he has to settle us down. Then you'll hear his cuss words. Just wait and see."

I was a bit dubious about this plan, but I did want to see the dignified Mr. Walker at his profane best. So Earl and I kept his poor father running back and forth like a yo-yo for over an hour. And as predicted, he became more intense and hostile each time he returned to our bedroom. I was getting very nervous and would have called off the demonstration, but Earl had been through it all before. He kept telling me, "It won't be long now."

Finally, about midnight, it happened. Mr. Walker's patience expired. He came thundering down the hall toward our room, shaking the entire house as his feet pounded the floor. He burst through the bedroom door and leaped on Earl's bed, flailing at the boy who was safely buried beneath three or four layers of blankets. Then from his lips came a stream of words that had seldom reached my tender ears. I was shocked, but Earl was delighted.

Even while his father was whacking the covers with his hand and screaming his profanity, Earl raised up and shouted to me, "Didja hear em? Huh? Didn't I tell ya? I tolja he would say it!" It's a wonder that Mr. Walker didn't kill his son at that moment!

I lay awake that night thinking about the episode and made up my mind *never* to let a child manipulate me like that when I grew up. Don't you see how important disciplinary techniques are to a child's respect for his parents? When a forty-five-pound bundle of trouble can deliberately reduce his powerful mother or father to a trembling, snarling mass of frustrations, then something changes in their relationship. Something precious is lost. The child develops an attitude of contempt which is certain to erupt during the stormy adolescent years to come. I sincerely wish every adult understood that simple characteristic of human nature.

Near my home in Arcadia, California, is a tan gentleman who certainly understands the way children think. He owns and operates Bud Lyndon's Swim School. Mr. Lyndon must be approaching sixty years of age now, and he has been working with youngsters most of his life. He has a remarkable comprehension of the principles of discipline, and I enjoy sitting at poolside just to watch the man work. However, there are few child developmentalists who could explain why he is so successful with the little swimmers in his pool. He is not soft and delicate in his manner; in fact, he tends to be somewhat gruff. When the kids get out of line he splashes water in their faces and says sternly, "Who told you to move? Stay where I put you until I ask you to swim!" He calls the boys "Men of Tomorrow," and other pet names. His class is regimented and every minute is utilized purposefully. But would you believe it, the children *love* Bud Lyndon. Why? Because they know that he loves them. Within his gruff manner is a message of affection that might escape the adult observer. Mr. Lyndon never embarrasses a child intentionally, and he "covers" for the youngster who swims more poorly. He delicately balances his authority with a subtle affection that attracts children like the Pied Piper. Mr. Bud Lyndon understands the meaning of discipline with love.

When I was in the ninth grade I had an athletic coach who affected me the same way. He was the master of the moment, and no one *dared* challenge his authority. I would have fought wild lions before tackling Mr. Ayers. Yes, I feared him. We all did. But he never abused his power. He treated me courteously and respectfully at a time when I needed all of the dignity I could get. Combined with his acceptance of the individual was an obvious self-confidence and ability to lead a pack of adolescent wolves who had devoured less capable teachers. And that's why my ninth-grade gym coach had a greater influence on me than any other person during my fifteenth year. Mr. Craig Ayers understood discipline with love.

Not every parent can be like Mr. Lyndon or Mr. Ayers, and I would not suggest that they try. Nor would it be wise for a mother to display the same gruffness at home that is appropriate on the athletic field or at the pool. Each person must fit his approach to discipline within his own personality patterns and the responses that feel natural. However, the overriding principle remains the same for men and women, mothers and fathers, coaches and teachers, pediatricians and psychologists: it involves discipline with love, a reasonable introduction to responsibility and self-control, parental leadership with a minimum of anger, respect for the dignity and worth of the child, realistic boundaries that are enforced with confident firmness, and a judicious use of rewards and punishment to those who challenge and resist. It is a system that bears the approval of the Creator Himself.

QUESTIONS

Question: It's easy for you to tell me not to get angry at my children, but there are times when they just make me furious. For example, I have a horrible time getting my ten-year-old daughter ready to catch the school bus each morning. She will get up when I insist, but she dawdles and plays as soon as I leave the room. I have to goad and push and warn her every few minutes or else she will be late. So

I get more and more angry, and usually end up by screaming insults at her. I know this is not the best way to handle
the little brat, but I declare, she makes me want to clobber
her. Tell me how I can get her moving without this emotion
every day.

Answer: You are playing right into your daughter's hands
by assuming the responsibility for getting her ready each
morning. A ten-year-old should definitely be able to handle
that task on her own steam, but your anger is not likely to
bring it about. We had a very similar problem with our own
daughter last year. Perhaps the solution we worked out
will be helpful to you.

Danae's morning time problem related primarily to her
compulsivity about her room. She will not leave for school
each day unless her bed is made perfectly and every trinket
is in its proper place. This was not something we taught
her; she has always been very meticulous about her possessions. (I should add that her brother, Ryan, does not have
that problem.) Danae could easily finish these tasks on time
if she were motivated to do so, but she was never in a particular hurry. Therefore, my wife began to fall into the same
habit you described, warning, threatening, pushing, shov-
ing, and ultimately becoming angry as the clock moved
toward the deadline.

Shirley and I discussed the problem and agreed that there
had to be a better method of getting through the morning.
I subsequently created a system which we called "Checkpoints." It worked like this. Danae was instructed to be
out of bed and standing erect before 6:30 each morning. It
was her responsibility to set her own clock-radio and get
herself out of bed. If she succeeded in getting up on time
(even one minute later was considered a missed item) she
immediately went to the kitchen where a chart was taped
to the refrigerator door. She then circled "yes" or "no,"

with regard to the first checkpoint for that date. It couldn't be more simple. She either did or did not get up by 6:30.

The second checkpoint occurred forty minutes later at 7:10. By that time, she was required to have her room straightened to her own satisfaction, be dressed and have her teeth brushed, hair combed, etc., and be ready to begin practicing the piano. Forty minutes was ample time for these tasks, which could actually be done in ten or fifteen minutes if she wanted to hurry. Thus, the only way she could miss the second checkpoint was to ignore it deliberately.

Now, what meaning did the checkpoints have? Did failure to meet them bring anger and wrath and gnashing of teeth? Of course not. The consequences were straightforward and fair. If Danae missed one checkpoint, she was required to go to bed thirty minutes earlier than usual that evening. If she missed two, she hit the "lily whites" an hour before her assigned hour. She was permitted to read during that time in bed, but she could not watch television or talk on the telephone. This procedure took all the morning pressure off Shirley and placed it on our daughter's shoulders, where it belonged. There were occasions when my wife got up just in time to fix breakfast, only to find Danae sitting soberly at the piano, clothed and in her right mind.

This system of discipline can serve as a model for parents who have similar behavioral problems with their children. It was not oppressive; in fact, Danae seemed to enjoy having a target to shoot at. The limits of acceptable performance were defined beyond question. The responsibility was clearly placed on the child. Consequences of noncompliance were fair and easily administered. And it required no adult anger or foot stamping.

There is an adaptation of this concept available to resolve the thorny conflicts in *your* home, too. The only limit lies in the creativity and imagination of the parent.

Question: What other errors do parents commonly make in disciplining their children?

Answer: For one thing, it is very easy to fall into the habit of saying "no" to our children.

"No, you can't go outside."

"No, you can't have a cookie."

"No, you can't use the telephone."

"No, you can't spend the night with a friend."

We parents could have answered affirmatively to all of these requests, but chose almost automatically to respond in the negative. Why? Because we didn't take time to stop and think about the consequences; because the activity could cause us more work or strain; because there could be danger in the request; because our children ask for a thousand favors a day and we find it convenient to refuse them all.

While every child needs to be acquainted with denial of some of his more extravagant wishes, there is also a need for parents to consider each request on its own merit. There are so many necessary "no's" in life that we should say "yes" whenever we can.

Dr. Fitzhugh Dodson extended this idea in his book *How to Father*. He wrote of the need for positive interactions with a child when the parent is not demanding anything of him.

> Analyze how your child sees you: is 99 percent of your role one in which you are expecting something of him, reminding him to do something, scolding him to stop doing something, or getting after him for misbehaving? If so, you are not building a deep positive emotional relationship. He needs time with you when you are not demanding anything from him, time when the

two of you are mutually enjoying yourselves. And he especially needs this time in the first five years of his life, because these are the years for building this kind of relationship with your child. Most abnormal rebellions of adolescents could have been prevented if the father had spent time building a deep and close relationship during the preschool years.[5]

Question: My husband and I are missionaries and have recently been assigned to a remote area of Colombia. Our ministry will be with an Indian culture which can only be reached by horseback or on foot. My concern is for our children, ages seven and nine, and their educational future. There are no schools near our new location, of course, and the nearest boarding facility will be more than 200 miles away. Because of the cost of travel, we would only be able to see them through the summers and perhaps at one other time during the year. Although I could teach them the academic subjects required between now and high school years, they obviously need social contact with their peers and we don't want to deprive them of those experiences. Would you recommend keeping them with us, or sending them away to school?

Answer: "What will we do with the children?" That is often the most difficult question missionaries must answer. I don't propose to have final solutions to this thorny problem, although I do have some definite views on the subject. I've dealt with the children of missionaries, many of whom had become bitter and resentful of the sacrifices they were required to make. They were deprived of a secure home at a critical stage in their development and experienced deep emotional wounds in the process. Consequently, adolescent rebellion was common among these angry young people who resented their parents and the God who sent them abroad.

Based on these observations, it is my firm conviction that the family unit of missionaries should remain intact, if at all possible. I cannot overemphasize the importance of parental support and love during the formative years of life. A child's sense of security and well-being is primarily rooted in the stability of his home and family. Therefore, he is certain to be shaken by separation not only from his parents, but also from his friends and the familiar surroundings of his own culture. He suddenly finds himself in a lonely dormitory in a foreign land where he may face rejection and pressures that threaten to overwhelm him. I can think of no better method of producing emotional (and spiritual) problems in a vulnerable child!

My friend Dr. Paul Cunningham expressed a similar view during a recent conference on family life. His comments were recorded by a court reporter and are quoted below, with Dr. Cunningham's permission:

> I am married to a missionary's daughter who at the age of five and a half was sent to boarding school in Africa, where she saw her parents about three times a year. This represents the most severe kind of sacrifice that a missionary has to face. I have had the privilege of ministering to the children of missionaries, and I think it can be safely said, and I want to say this very carefully, that those children who have had this experience often never fully recover from it.
>
> My wife, for example, was "put down" when she was in the school because of the strong anti-American sentiment there. She was the only American in her school. We're not talking about a child ten or twelve years old, but only six. All in all, it has made her a tre-

mendously strong person, and I doubt if she would have been all that she is to me and to our children had she not had those tough experiences. But at the same time, were she not from strong English stock with tremendous gifts and graces, I don't know . . . maybe she would not have survived, because others haven't.

I can't feel that this is a good policy at this point to make this the only answer for these families . . . to separate tender little children from their parents. I know of one situation, for example, where the children have to take a long ride in a riverboat to see their parents; I'm talking about little children. It's a trip of several hours to their mission compound. Their mother says goodbye to them in the fall, and she does not see them for many months because of the expense of traveling. They could be taken by helicopter instead of the riverboat ride, but they don't have the money. We must do something to assist people like this, whatever the cost.

Dr. Cunningham and I agree that the true issue may actually be one of priorities. Meaningful family involvement outranks educational considerations by a wide margin, in my view. Furthermore, contact with parents during the early years is even more important than contact with peers. And finally, even missionaries (who have been called to a life of sacrifice and service) must reserve some of their resources for their own families. After all, a lifetime of successes on a foreign field will be rather pale and insignificant to those who lose their own children.

Question: Are you acquainted with a little booklet for parents, entitled, *Children, Fun or Frenzy?* If so, would you comment on its recommendations for discipline of children?

Answer: Yes, I am familiar with that booklet, written by Pat Fabrizio. Many thousands of copies of this publication have been distributed or sold within the Christian community. In it (and in a similar publication entitled *Why Daddy Loves to Come Home*) Mrs. Fabrizio relates her own experiences as a permissive mother whose children were undisciplined and disrespectful. Through a process of struggle she and her husband discovered biblical principles of discipline which resulted in a turning point in their home.

Some valuable concepts are included in this booklet, and I would not condemn it. But I am concerned about Mrs. Fabrizio's undue emphasis on corporal punishment. While she was permissive and wishy-washy in the first instance, she seemed to become obsessed with the necessity of spanking in the second. Thus, it would appear to me that the author went from one extreme to another in her philosophy of child rearing. Let me quote her writings:

". . . *every time* (Fabrizio's italics) I ask my child to do anything, either, "Come here," "Don't touch," "Hush," "Put that down," or whatever it is, I must see that he obeys. When I have said it once in a normal tone, if he does not obey immediately, I *must* (italics mine) take up a switch and spank him (love demands this) enough to hurt so he will not want it repeated."

In another instance, she wrote of the necessity of spanking for the "slightest disobedience" and continued, "no matter the nature of the circumstance of the offense, the correction is always the same because the wrongdoing is always one of disobedience."

Likewise, Mrs. Fabrizio describes a spanking that she administered because her daughter, "intended to obey me, but she got busy playing and forgot." These are classic examples of overextending a healthy biblical principle to the point of danger. A spanking should come only in response to deliberate defiance, in my view. It should be the parental reaction to a child's "I will not!" But how unwise to spank a youngster for forgetting! I am even more distressed by an illustration describing an evening when Mr. and Mrs. Fabrizio failed to discipline their naughty toddler before sending him to bed.

> So Daddy went in and woke him. He sat him on his lap until he was thoroughly awake and then told him that Daddy did not have peace about the incident and confessed to him that we had not been obeying the Lord in being sure that he obeyed us. Daddy told him that he would have to spank him because he did not obey. So he spanked him and put him back to bed.[6]

Can you imagine what this was like from a child's perspective? He was awakened out of a sound sleep and spanked for something that happened hours before! A twenty-month-old child can hardly remember his actions from one moment to the next; the events of yesterday are a gray memory. His guilt-ridden father "confessed to him that (he) had not been obeying the Lord." How frightening! What better way is there to give a child nightmares than never to know when the Lord will send Daddy in to spank him for some behavior that was tolerated yesterday?

The reason this booklet frustrates me is that the central message is so badly needed. Children must be taught respect and responsibility. They must be brought under parental authority. And *most* of them need to be spanked now and then. But we are not limited to one disciplinary technique, nor will a single formula fit every situation or every human being. There will be times when a child should be required to spend ten minutes sitting on a chair, as suggested earlier. Or a privilege may be taken away or the child may be sent to bed an hour early. There are many measures which should be varied to fit the offense and the circumstances. And occasionally, I have found it useful to talk to a repentant child and grant him unexpected and undeserved mercy. My point is that children are infinitely complex, and their leadership requires tact, cunning, courage, skill, and knowledge.

Ultimately, the key to competent parenthood is in being able to get behind the eyes of your child, seeing what he sees and feeling what he feels. When he is lonely, he needs your company. When he is defiant, he needs your help in controlling his impulses. When he is afraid, he needs the security of your embrace. When he is curious, he needs your patient instruction. When he is happy, he needs to share his laughter and joy with those he loves.

Thus, the parent who intuitively comprehends his child's feelings is in a position to respond appropriately and meet the needs that are apparent. And at this point, raising healthy children becomes a highly developed art, requiring the greatest wisdom, patience, devotion and love that God has given to us. The Apostle Paul called the Christian life a "reasonable service." We parents would do well to apply that sane standard to the behavior of our children.

I don't want to be too critical of Mrs. Fabrizio's writings, for it is apparent that she seeks to implement biblical principles which we both love and trust. However, overzealousness with children can be a dangerous virtue. You see, it is extremely important that boys and girls understand the purpose of punishment and perceive it as reasonable and deserved. When spankings are given routinely for the "slightest disobedience," then lasting resentment can be generated which sets the stage for later adolescent explosions.

Question: You have discussed child abuse and the anger

of parents. Would you comment further on the violence in our society at large, and the forces which are propelling it?

Answer: There are few subjects that cause me greater concern than the exposure being given to crime and violence in America today. Only yesterday, a squadron of Los Angeles police cornered a desperate gunman in a residential area of the community. The fugitive had barricaded himself in a small house, and held three juvenile hostages inside. Television crews were on hand to photograph one of the children, a teen-aged boy, as he was forced outside and then shot in the head by his abductor, who subsequently committed suicide. The pathetic young victim died on the sidewalk in a pool of his own blood. I sat stunned, literally sick to my stomach, while the drama was broadcast in full color last night.

A flood of emotions ran through my mind as I gazed into the immobile, unfocused eyes of the dying adolescent. Mixed with deep pity and remorse was a sudden outpouring of indignation—a revulsion which has been accumulating for years. I was angry at the profiteers who have nurtured violence in our society, and at those millions who seem to thrive on it; I was angry at movie producers like Sam Peckinpah, who have smeared blood and guts all over the silver screen; I was angry at theater patrons for demanding a dozen disembowelments per hour in their visual entertainment; I was angry at television networks for giving us continuous police stories, with their guns and silly automobile chases and karate chops and SWAT teams. I was angry at the Supreme Court for legalizing 900,000 abortions by American women last year; I was angry at the Palestine Liberation Army for killing eight innocent athletes at the Olympic Games in Munich; I was angry at Truman Capote for writing *In Cold Blood,* and at his thrill-seeking readers for wanting to know how a peaceful family was mercilessly butchered on their farm; and I was particularly angry at the pathetic system of American justice which makes crime so profitable and punishment so improbable.

But my indignation will change nothing and the wave of violence and lawlessness will continue unabated. We have become so desensitized to human suffering and exploitation that even the most horrible events are accepted as part of our regular evening "entertainment" on the tube.

I think it is time that millions of decent, law-abiding citizens rise up with one voice to oppose the industries that are profiting from violence. A valiant campaign of this nature was waged in 1977 by the National Parent Teacher Association, directing their efforts at television networks and companies that support the most damaging programs. Of course, this pressure from the PTA brought an anguished cry of "foul play" from the greedy profiteers whose pockets were lined with bloodstained money. Nevertheless, Sears Roebuck, Union Oil, and other large companies pledged to sponsor no more violent programs on television. This form of economic sanction is the most powerful tool available to influence our free enterprise system, and we should use it incisively against those who would destroy us from within. We have sat on our hands long enough!

Question: How do you feel about the Equal Rights Amendment which is being supported by the women's movement?

Answer: I am in favor of constitutional rights for both women and men, but I am unalterably opposed to this amendment. Why? Because the wording is so nebulous that the ultimate interpretation of its meaning will be made by the nation's judicial system. And frankly, I don't trust the judges to whom the legal issues will be appealed. I've seen their handiwork during the past ten years, and shudder to think that the future of our families may depend on their decisions. America's homes are too important to risk annihilation in the Federal courts. Anything that threatens this foundation of democracy must be viewed with alarm. Mine is not a popular view, but I feel it strongly.

5 The Scourge of Sibling Rivalry

In a recent book I described an episode that best expresses the frustration of parenthood. It happened when our son, Ryan, was four months old and my wife put him on the dressing table to change his diapers. As soon as she removed his wet garments, he made like a fountain and sprayed the wall and the carpet and a picture of Little Boy Blue. Shirley had no sooner repaired the damage when the telephone rang; while she was gone, Ryan was struck by a sudden attack of projectile diarrhea, and he machine-gunned his crib and the rest of the nursery. By the time my patient wife bathed her son and scoured the room, she was near exhaustion. She dressed Ryan in clean, sweet-smelling clothes and put him over her shoulder affectionately. At that moment, he deposited his breakfast down her neck and into her undergarments. When I arrived home from work that evening, I found Shirley sitting in a darkened corner of the family room, muttering quietly to herself and slowly shaking her head from side to side.

Such is the price of procreation. (One father described his infant son as "a noise at one end and a mess at the other.") I think it is time for us to admit that being a mother or father is not only one of life's greatest joys, but it can also represent a personal sacrifice and challenge. Everything of value is expensive, and children are no exception to the rule. On the other hand, I am also convinced that many of the frustrations of raising children result from our failure to plan and organize and understand the issues. Few problems of parenthood are new or unique; we have all experienced similar difficulties. And there are better ways of coping. Let's take a fresh look, then, at two of these universal stress points in this chapter and the next.

Bitter Brothers and Surly Sisters

If American women were asked to indicate *the* most irritating feature of child rearing, I'm convinced that sibling rivalry would get their unanimous vote. Little children (and older ones too) are not content just to hate each other in private. They attack one another like miniature warriors, mobilizing their troops and probing for a weakness in the defensive line. They argue, hit, kick, scream, grab toys, taunt, tattle, and sabotage the opposing forces. I knew one child who deeply resented being sick with a cold while his older sibling was healthy, so he secretly blew his nose on the mouthpiece of his brother's musical instrument! The big loser from such combat, of course, is the harassed mother who must listen to the noise of the battlefield and then try to patch up the wounded. If her emotional nature requires peace and tranquillity (and most women do) she may stagger under the barrage of cannonfire.

Columnist Ann Landers recently asked her readers to respond to the question, "If you had known then what you know now, would you had children?" Among ten thousand women who answered, 70 percent said No! A subsequent survey by *Good Housekeeping* posed the same question and 95 percent of the respondents answered Yes. It is impossible to explain the contradictory results from these two inquiries, although the accompanying comments were enlightening. One unidentified woman wrote, "Would I have children again? A thousand times, NO! My children have completely destroyed my life, my marriage, and my identity as a person. There are no joys. Prayers don't help— nothing stops a 'screaming kid.' "

It is my contention that something *will* stop a screaming kid, or even a dozen of them. It is not necessary or healthy to allow children to destroy each other and make life miserable for the adults around them. Sibling rivalry is difficult to "cure" but it can certainly be treated. Toward that objective, let me offer three suggestions which should be helpful in achieving a state of armistice at home.

1. *Don't Inflame the Natural Jealousy of Children.*

Sibling rivalry is not new, of course. It was responsible for the first murder on record (when Cain killed Abel), and has been represented in virtually every two-child family from that time to this. The underlying source of this conflict is old-fashioned jealousy and competition between children. Marguerite and Willard Beecher, writing in their book *Parents on the Run,* expressed the inevitability of this struggle as follows:

> It was once believed that if parents would explain to a child that he was having a little brother or sister, he would not resent it. He was told that his parents had enjoyed him so much that they wanted to increase their happiness. This was supposed to avoid jealous competition and rivalry. It did not work. Why should it? Needless to say, if a man tells his wife he has loved her so much that he now plans to bring another wife into the home to "increase his happiness," she would not be immune to jealousy. On the contrary, the fight would just begin—in exactly the same fashion as it does with children.[1]

If jealousy is so common, then how can parents minimize the natural antagonism which children feel for their siblings? The first step is to avoid circumstances which compare them unfavorably with each other. Lecturer Bill Gothard has stated that the root of all feelings of inferiority is *comparison.* I agree. The question is not "How am I doing?" It is "How am I doing compared with John or Steven or Marion?" The issue is not how fast can I run, but who crosses the finish line first. A boy does not care how tall he is; he is vitally interested in "who is tallest." Each child systematically measures himself against his peers, and is tremendously sensitive to failure within his own family.

Accordingly, parents should guard against comparative statements which routinely favor one child over another.

Jim Dobson, Danae, and Ryan on vacation in Colorado

Jim Dobson in his study at home

Shirley returning home from a successful shopping trip

▲ *The Dobson's strong-willed dachshund, Siggie.*
▼ *Danae at eleven years of age*

Ryan on horseback at five years of age

The Dobson family at the kitchen table

▲ *Dr. Dobson greeting those to whom he has just spoken*

▼ *Danae and Ryan with their dad, photographed in their backyard treehouse.*

Shirley Dobson at a recent Sweetheart Banquet, when she was asked to wear her wedding dress, originally worn August 27, 1960.

This is particularly true in three areas. First, children are extremely sensitive about the matter of physical attractiveness and body characteristics. It is highly inflammatory to commend one child at the expense of the other. Suppose, for example, that Sharon is permitted to hear the casual remark about her sister, "Betty is sure going to be a gorgeous girl." The very fact that Sharon was not mentioned will probably establish the two girls as rivals. If there is a significant difference in beauty between the two, you can be assured that Sharon has already concluded, "'Yeah, I'm the ugly one." When her fears are then confirmed by her parents, resentment and jealousy are generated.

Beauty is *the* most significant factor in the self-esteem of Western children, as I attempted to express in *Hide or Seek*. Anything that a parent utters on this subject within the hearing of children should be screened carefully. It has the power to make brothers and sisters hate one another.

Second, the matter of intelligence is another sensitive nerve to be handled with care. It is not uncommon to hear parents say in front of their children, "I think the younger boy is actually brighter than his brother." Adults find it difficult to comprehend how powerful that kind of assessment can be in a child's mind. Even when the comments are unplanned and are spoken routinely, they convey how a child is "seen" within his family. We are all vulnerable to that bit of evidence.

Third, children (and especially boys) are extremely competitive with regard to athletic abilities. Those who are slower, weaker, and less coordinated than their brothers are rarely able to accept "second best" with grace and dignity. Consider, for example, the following note given to me by the mother of two boys. It was written by her nine-year-old son to his eight-year-old brother, the evening after the younger child had beaten him in a race.

Dear Jim:

I am the greatest and your the badest. And I can beat everybody in a race and you can't beat anybody in a race. I'm the smartest and your the dumbest. I'm the best sport player and your the badest sport player. And your also a hog. I can beat anybody up. And that's the truth. And that's the end of this story.

Yours truly,

Richard

This note is humorous to me, because Richard's motive was so poorly disguised. He had been badly stung by his humiliation on the field of honor, so he came home and raised the battle flags. He will probably spend the next eight weeks looking for opportunities to fire torpedos into Jim's soft underbelly. Such is the nature of mankind.

Am I suggesting, then, that parents eliminate all aspects of individuality within family life or that healthy competition should be discouraged? Definitely not. I am saying that in matters relative to beauty, brains, and athletic ability, each child should know that in his parents' eyes, he is respected and has equal worth with his siblings. Praise and criticism *at home* should be distributed as evenly as possible, although some children will inevitably be more successful in the outside world. And finally, we should remember that children do not build fortresses around strengths—they construct them to protect weakness. Thus, when a child like Richard begins to brag and boast and attack his siblings, he is revealing the threats he feels at that point. Our sensitivity to those signals will help minimize the potential for jealousy within our children.

2. *Establish a Workable System of Justice.*

Sibling rivalry is also at its worst when there is no reasonable system of justice in the home—where the "lawbreakers" do not get caught, or if apprehended are set free without standing trial. It is important to understand that laws in a society are established and enforced for the purpose of protecting people from each other. Likewise, a family is a mini-society with the same requirement for protection of human rights.

For purposes of illustration, suppose that I live in a community where there is no established law. Policemen do not exist and there are no courts to whom disagreements can be appealed. Under those circumstances, my neighbor and I can abuse each other with impunity. He can take my lawnmower and throw rocks through my windows, while I steal the peaches from his favorite tree and dump my leaves over his fence. This kind of mutual antagonism has a way of escalating day by day, becoming ever more violent with the passage of time. When permitted to run its natural course, as in early American history, the end result can be feudal hatred and murder.

As indicated, individual families are similar to societies in their need for law and order. In the absence of justice, "neighboring" siblings begin to assault one another. The older child is bigger and tougher, which allows him to oppress his younger brothers and sisters. But the junior member of the family is not without weapons of his own. He strikes back by breaking the toys and prized possessions of the older sibling and interferes when friends are visiting. Mutual hatred then erupts like an angry volcano, spewing its destructive contents on everyone in its path.

Nevertheless, when the children appeal to their parents for intervention, they are often left to fight it out among themselves. In many homes, the parents do not have sufficient disciplinary control to enforce their judgments. In others, they are so exasperated with constant bickering among siblings that they refuse to get involved. In still others, parents require an older child to live with an admitted injustice "because your brother is smaller than you." Thus, they tie his hands and render him utterly defenseless against the mischief of his bratty little brother or sister. Even more commonly today, mothers and fathers are both working while their children are at home busily disassembling each other.

I will say it again to parents: one of your most important responsibilities is to establish an equitable system of justice and a balance of power at home. There should be reasonable "laws" which are enforced fairly for each member of the family. For purposes of illustration, let me list the boundaries and rules which have evolved through the years in my own home.

1. Neither child is *ever* allowed to make fun of the other in a destructive way. Period! This is an inflexible rule with no exceptions.

2. Each child's room is his private territory. There are locks on both doors, and permission to enter is a revokable privilege. (Families with more than one child in each bedroom can allocate available living space for each youngster.)

3. The older child is not permitted to tease the younger child.

4. The younger child is forbidden to harass the older child.

5. The children are not required to play with each other when they prefer to be alone or with other friends.

6. We mediate any genuine conflict as quickly as possible, being careful to show impartiality and extreme fairness.

As with any plan of justice, this plan requires (1) respect for leadership of the parent, (2) willingness by the parent to mediate, (3) occasional enforcement or punishment. When this approach is accomplished with love, the emotional tone of the home can be changed from one of hatred to (at least) tolerance.

3. *Recognize That the Hidden "Target" of Sibling Rivalry Is You.*

It would be naive to miss the true meaning of sibling conflict: it often represents a form of manipulation of parents. Quarreling and fighting provide an opportunity for both children to "capture" adult attention. It has been written, "Some children had rather be wanted for murder than not wanted at all." Toward this end, a pair of obnoxious kids can tacitly agree to bug their parents until they get a response—even if it is an angry reaction.

One father told me recently that his son and his nephew began to argue and then beat each other with their fists. Both fathers were nearby and decided to let the fight run its natural course. During the first lull in the action one of the boys glanced sideways toward the passive men and said, "Isn't anybody going to stop us before we get hurt?!" The fight, you see, was something neither boy wanted. Their violent combat was directly related to the presence of the two adults and would have taken a different form if the boys had been alone. Children will often "hook" their parents' attention and intervention in this way.

Believe it or not, this form of sibling rivalry is easiest to control. The parent must simply render the behavior unprofitable to each participant. Instead of wringing their hands and crying and begging and screaming (which actually reinforces the disruptive behavior and makes it worse), a mother or father should approach the conflict with dignity and self-control.

I would recommend that a modified version of the following "speech" be given to quarreling children, depending on the age and circumstances: "Tommy and Chuck, I want you to sit in these chairs and give me your complete attention. Now you both know that you have been harassing and irritating each other all through the morning. Tommy, you knocked over the castle that Chuck was building, and Chuck, you messed up Tommy's hair. So every few minutes I've found myself telling you to quit quarreling. Well, I'm not angry at you, because all brothers fight like that, but I am telling you that I'm tired of hearing it. I have important things to do, and I can't take the time to be separating a couple of scratching cats every few minutes.

"Now listen carefully. If the two of you want to pick on each other and make yourselves miserable, then be my guest [assuming there is a fairly equal balance of power between them]. Go outside and fight until you're exhausted. But it's not going to occur under my feet anymore. It's over! And you know that I mean business when I make that kind of statement. Do we understand each other?"

Would that implied warning end the conflict? Of course not—at least, not the first time. It would be necessary to deliver on the promise of "action." Having made the boundaries clear, I would act decisively the *instant* either boy returned to his bickering. If I had separate bedrooms, I would confine one child to each room for at least thirty minutes of complete boredom—without radio or television. Or I would assign one to clean the garage and the other to mow the lawn. Or I would make them take a nap. My avowed purpose would be to make them believe me the next time I offered a suggestion for peace and tranquillity.

It is simply not necessary to permit children to destroy the joy in living, as expressed by the frustrated mother to *Good Housekeeping*. And what is most surprising, children are the happiest when their parents enforce these reasonable limits with love and dignity.

QUESTIONS

Question: We are planning our family very carefully, and want to space the children properly. Is there an ideal age span that will bring greater harmony between them?

Answer: Children who are two years apart and of the same sex are more likely to be competitive with one another. On the other hand, they are also more likely to enjoy mutual companionship. If you produce your babies four or more years apart there will be less camaraderie between them but at least you'll have only one child in college at a time. My evasive reply to your question reflects my personal bias: There are many more important reasons for planning a baby at a particular time than the age of those already born. Of greater significance is the health of the mother, the desire for another child, financial considerations, and the stability of the marriage. The relative ages of siblings is not one of the major determiners, in my opinion.

Question: (The following excerpt was taken from an actual letter sent to me by a creative mother.)

You recommended in *Dare to Discipline* and *Hide or Seek* that we use a monetary reward system to encourage our children to accept new responsibilities. This approach has helped a great deal and our family is functioning much smoother. However, I had an idea for improving the system which has worked beautifully with my two boys, ages six and eight. In order for them to earn a reward for brushing their teeth, making their bed, putting away their clothes, etc., they *both* must complete the jobs as assigned. In other words, I tax them both for one child's failure and reward them both for mutual successes. They got in the spirit of the game immediately, cooperating with one another and working together to achieve the goal. It has made them business partners, in a sense. I thought you would be interested in this approach.

Answer: This mother has done what I hope other parents will do: use my writings as a springboard to creative approaches of their own. My illustrations merely show that the most successful parents are those who find unique solutions to the routine problems of living. The writer of this letter has done that beautifully.

Question: You referred to siblings who manipulate their mothers and fathers. On the other hand, isn't the parent "manipulating" the child by the use of rewards and negative consequences?

Answer: No more than a factory supervisor is manipulating his employees by insisting that they arrive at work by 9 A.M. No more than a policeman manipulates the speeding driver by giving him a traffic ticket. No more than an insurance company manipulates that same driver by increasing his premium. The word "manipulation" implies a sinister or selfish motive. I prefer the term *leadership,* which is in the best interest of everyone concerned—even when it involves unpleasant consequences.

Question: Thank you for admitting that children can be terribly frustrating to parents. It helps just to hear that other mothers have felt the same desire to run—to escape to some quiet place. I think I can do a better job by knowing that I'm not the only woman in the world who occasionally feels inadequate for the task of raising children.

Answer: I receive many comments similar to yours from mothers who have trouble coping with domestic responsibilities. One woman wrote, "I finally got it all together but I can't remember where I left it!" We obviously live in a very hectic period of American history, where fatigue and time pressure are our worst enemies. But running away usually offers no lasting solutions because the problems are *within us* rather than being imposed from the outside. Whenever I hear someone talk simplistically about running from their problems, I'm reminded of the man who concluded during the 1930s that the world was about to disintegrate. Thus, he packed his belongings and moved to the loneliest spot he could find in the South Pacific—a forgotten little island called Guadalcanal. And, of course, he woke up a few years later to find World War II in his front yard. It is very difficult to avoid our problems on this shrinking earth.

I received some desperate mail from people who have fled in the night to escape intolerable frustration at home. Consider the words of the mother who recently wrote the following S.O.S. from an unidentified Holiday Inn.

August 20, 1976

Dear Dr. Dobson:

I am writing you from this motel because I have "run away" from my loving husband, my six-year-old daughter (Annie) and my five-month-old son (Paulie). My little girl is a beautiful blonde with blue eyes, but she throws temper tantrums and irritates me to the breaking point. My son seems to cry twenty-four hours a day. I need one uninterrupted night's sleep so badly.

I've tried so hard to be a good mother and wife . . . a good neighbor and Christian daughter. I've wanted to meet my responsibilities to my family, but I'm completely exhausted. I became a monster this past week. I hit my daughter across the face, bruised her arm from shaking her so hard, yelled and screamed and cried, then wanted to die from guilt.

I've come here to try to get a hold of what's left of me but I don't think I can. I feel my prayers take too long to be answered, or else I don't recognize the answers when they come. When I'm home, there's not enough time to even brush my teeth, let alone pray about Annie's behavior and my inferiority as a parent. If I spank her she retorts, "That didn't even hurt" or she scratches, kicks, and pulls my hair. Yet when I left last night she sobbed for me not to go, despite my reassuring her that I would come back.

We spent $100 last month to take four counseling sessions on parenting techniques. Well, some of it works but some of it is too far removed from my child's misbehavior to do any good. Annie was hostile and aggressive even before Paulie arrived. I can't help wanting to get away from her. She spent a week with Grandma and went to Disneyland recently. I really felt guilty because I hardly missed her.

I just talked with my husband by telephone and he said Annie was having a temper tantrum. She wants to go find me and I don't even want to go home! I adore my husband. I've had little chance to show him how much, and I've been blessed with a daughter and son, both of whom I always wanted to have. The problem now is that I can't handle the "routine panic" of our lives. Next Thursday will be my 28th birthday. Please help me.

Mrs. J. S.

Unfortunately, Mrs. J. S. did not include her return address in her letter and I had no way to contact her. I have often wondered if she received the help she was so desperately seeking in that distant motel.

Perhaps it would be constructive to include another letter which arrived the same week as the one above, expressing a very different kind of despair. It came from Oxford, England, and the writer gave me permission to quote her words of frustration:

Dear Dr. Dobson:

I have just read your book *What Wives Wish Their Husbands Knew About Women,* and was very helped by it. It is one of the best books I have ever read. But, please, why don't you authors ever write for people like me?

Why is nothing written for women who are barren; who desperately long for a child of their own but do not have one. Why don't you help us to live with the feeling of being an incomplete woman, to cope with relatives and friends having babies and rearing their families while you have nothing; to cope with the veiled pressure from family to provide grandchildren for your parents (which you would love to do if only you could); to beat the deep, terrible depressions when finally you become pregnant (twice) only to lose both in miscarriages. To exist around Christmas when *everything's* geared to children and it all just gets unbearable (so that last year I took an overdose of drugs to try and escape it). To look forward hopefully to the future, when there seems to be little to plan for or look forward to.

I know Christ can help; but why don't *people?* Why does society imply that a marriage isn't fulfilled without children, and so add to the guilt and unhappiness?

Why don't people like you ever write books to help people like us?

Yours,

Mrs. R. K.

Mrs. K. is absolutely right. The world seems designed for children and those who produce them. We who have been blessed by little ones should be sensitive to the feelings of those like this woman who value motherhood more than life itself. Human kindness would go a long way toward easing their distress, if we weren't so busy thinking of ourselves. I wish I could get the writer of the first letter together with the author of the second. A fascinating (and helpful?) conversation might develop between them.

Question: I am a single mother and am worried about my seven-year-old son. There are no male members of my family living nearby, so my boy is growing up in a world of women. I am also concerned about how to discipline him. What can I do?

Answer: Your question touches an increasingly important aspect of parenthood in America today. There are vast numbers of divorced or widowed mothers and fathers who struggle with the responsibilities of solitary parenthood. The U.S. Census Bureau reports that households headed by singles under thirty-four increased 55 percent between 1970 and 1973! The upward trend continues to this moment, and its depressing effects are difficult to overstate. I particularly empathize with the single mother, such as yourself, who must arise early each morning, take her children to a child care center, work eight or nine hours at a job, then try to meet the physical, emotional, and spiritual needs of her youngsters at the end of the day when others are resting. It can't be done! Something will be shortchanged. There is simply not enough energy in the human body to work eighteen hours a day, every day, year in and year out. And as your question acknowledges, mothers don't make very good fathers and fathers are often lousy mothers.

Do I have a magic solution for the problem? No. Parenthood was designed to be a two-person job, and when the task falls to a single adult, enormous pressures are inevitable. I can offer two suggestions, however, which may be helpful with regard to the more specific question of masculine identification.

The first will require a small amount of money, but I believe it will be well invested. I would suggest that you call the nearest high school guidance office and ask to speak to the counselor of third or fourth year students. Then explain your need to "rent" a mature, athletic boy who can take your son to a park and teach him to throw a ball, cast a fishing line, or build a playhouse. Request the counselor's recommendation of a stable young man who is likely to enjoy working with a seven-year-old boy. Then pay this fellow the going hourly rate (for high school students) to spend two or three hours with your son each Saturday.

Second, it is clearly the task of the *church* to assist you with your parenting responsibilities. This requirement is implicit in Jesus' commandment that we love and support the needy in all walks of life. He said, "Inasmuch as ye do it unto the least of these, ye do it unto me." If Jesus meant these words, and He obviously did, then our effort on behalf of a fatherless or motherless child is seen by the Master of the universe as a direct service to Himself!

But the commandment to Christians is more explicitly stated in James 1:27: "The Christian who is pure and without fault, from God the Father's point of view, is the one who takes care of orphans and widows, and who remains true to the Lord." (TLB)

Perhaps you could xerox a copy of this page of my book and send it to the pastor of your church, asking if he knows a responsible father within his congregation who might take these scriptural commandments literally.

As to the larger question of discipline by a single parent, let me emphasize that the principles I have outlined remain the same even when the family constellation changes. Children still need discipline and love and stability and opportunity, just as they did when both parents were available to lead them. The only thing unique for the single parent is that the task becomes much more difficult and demanding. (I seriously doubt if any single parents really need me to tell them that!)

Let me recommend a book which may provide additional assistance. It is entitled *The Single Parent,* by Virginia Watts, and is published by Fleming H. Revell (1977). This Christian book provides an overview of the unique problems faced by a single mother or father, and offers some practical suggestions and insights.

Question: Would you comment on the views of Dr. Haim Ginott, who wrote *Between Parent and Child,* and *Between Parent and Teenager?*

Answer: The popular Dr. Ginott was very eloquent in teaching parents to understand and communicate with their children. No one has written more effectively on that subject than he. However, I don't believe he had any significant grasp of the principles of discipline. If you go through his books and lift out his statements relating to teaching respect and responsibility, all of his recommendations leaned in the direction of permissiveness. Consider the four paraphrased examples that follow.

Concerning Homework:

Dr. Ginott recommended that parents not assume *any* responsibility for overseeing children's homework. They were advised to remain uninvolved, even if a child blatantly chose to disregard his assignments and accept unnecessary failure. The only occasion when they should check or supervise the homework would be at the specific invitation of the student.

Concerning Routine Chores and Responsibilities:

It was Ginott's opinion that the assignment of routine chores at home could have a detrimental influence on the development of a child's character. Whereas daily obligations might produce cleaner houses and yards and contribute to obedience, Ginott felt the emotional consequences of these tasks were on the negative side of the ledger. Even when pets were adopted by the child, the parents were to retain responsibility for their care and maintenance.

Concerning Spankings:

As might be predicted, Ginott viewed spankings as an act of violence on the part of the parent. He felt this form of punishment gave children a taste of the jungle, and taught them to hit and abuse others. Instead of spankings, Ginott hoped that parents could find some civilized outlets for their *own* uncivilized emotions.

Concerning Public Rowdiness:

Ginott gave an example of a child who jumped on the sofa while he and his mother were visiting Aunt Mary. Incredibly, Ginott recommended that the mother ignore her bouncing son, leaving the discipline exclusively in the hands of Aunt Mary. His point was that children obey outsiders more readily than mothers and fathers who should be relieved of disciplinary responsibilities while in the homes of others.

Regarding this final example, can't you visualize the scene? Donnie is turning cartwheels on Auntie Mary's new sofa, while Mother sits passively as though she doesn't notice. Auntie's blood pressure is zinging up near 220 but she's too civilized to do what she's thinking. When she finally blows, she's liable to throw Donnie and his stoic momma right through the front door. Ginott didn't see it that way. He stated that the host has the responsibility to establish rules and enforce them in his own home. Let's suppose, as Ginott suggests, that Aunt Mary quietly takes the bouncing Donaldo by the neck and crams him into a chair in the corner. Then we would see some dramatic changes in Mom's blood pressure. The only one remaining cool in both instances is the little brat who was using the furniture as a trampoline.

No, Dr. Ginott had little understanding of the principles of discipline, from my point of view. His books do have other value, however.

6 The Problem of Hyperactivity

or
Jiggle, Jump,
Climb, and Roll
on the Floor

We should turn our attention now to the common problem of hyperactivity, which parents also find particularly distressing. A mother complained to me recently that her preschooler was like a human jet engine, flying at top velocity during every waking hour. She said trying to get him to hold still was like trying to sew a button on a poached egg. My deepest sympathies are with her. I have seen similar children in my practice who threatened to destroy my office during the course of a brief visit.

One such youngster was a seven-year-old boy named Kurt who was afflicted with Downs Syndrome (a form of mental retardation which was originally called mongolism). This little fellow was frantically active, and literally "attacked" my furniture when he entered the room. He scrambled over the top of my desk, knocking over pictures and files and paper weights. Then this lad grabbed for the telephone and held it in the direction of my ear. I humored him by faking a conversation with a mythical caller, but Kurt had other purposes in mind. He jumped from my desk and scurried into the office of a psychologist next door, insisting that my colleague play the same game. As it happened, our two phones were on the same extension, and this little seven-year-old boy had succeeded in outsmarting the two child development "experts." There we were, talking to each other on the phone without anything relevant to say. It was a humbling experience.

A truly hyperactive child can humble any adult, particularly if the disorder is not understood by his parent. His problem is certainly relevant to the theme of this book, since there are no more "strong-willed" children than those whose defiance and disobedience have an organic or emotional origin. Let's discuss the nature of this behavioral difficulty, then, and offer some suggestions for discipline and management of affected youngsters. Perhaps a question and answer format will allow us to present the topic most expeditiously.

What Is Hyperactivity?

Hyperactivity (also called hyperkinesis, minimal brain dysfunction, impulse disorder, and at least thirty other terms) is defined as excessive and *uncontrollable* movement. It usually involves distractibility, restlessness, and a short attention span. I italicized the word uncontrollable, because the severely affected child is absolutely incapable of sitting quietly in a chair or slowing down his level of activity. He is propelled from within by forces he can neither explain or ameliorate.

What Causes the Phenomenon?

Hyperactivity often appears related to damage to the central nervous system, although it can also be caused by emotional stress and fatigue. Some authorities believe that virtually all children born through the birth canal (that is, not by cesarean section) are likely to sustain damage to brain tissue during the birth process. The difference between patients who are severely affected (and are called cerebral palsied) and those who have no obvious symptoms may reflect three variables: (1) Where the damage is located; (2) How massive the lesion is; and (3) How quickly it occurred. Thus, it is possible that some hyperactive children were afflicted by an unidentified brain interference very early which caused no other symptoms or problems. I must emphasize, however, that this explanation is merely speculative and that the medical understanding of this disorder is far from complete.

How Can Damage to Brain Tissue Cause Frantic Activity in a Child?

Relatively little is known about the human brain and its malfunctions. I knew one neurologically impaired child, for example, who could read the words, "Go shut the door," with no understanding of the written command. However, if a tape recording was made while he read, "Go shut the door," this child could hear the replay of his own voice and understand the words perfectly. Another patient in a mental hospital could completely disassemble and repair complex television sets, yet did not have the common sense to handle the routine responsibilities of living outside a hospital setting. Another man, wounded in combat, had the sad characteristic of being unable to keep any thought to himself. He mumbled his innermost ideas, to the embarrassment and shock of everyone nearby.

Brain disorders are expressed in many strange ways, including the frenzy of hyperactivity. No one can explain exactly why it happens, other than the obvious fact that the electrochemical mechanisms which control body movement have been altered, resulting in excessive stimulation to the muscles.

How Can Anxiety or Emotional Problems Cause Hyperactivity?

When adults are under severe stress or anxiety, their inner tension is typically expressed in the form of physical activity. An expectant father "paces the floor," or smokes one cigarette after another, or his hands may tremble. A basketball coach will race up and down the sidelines while the outcome of the game is in doubt. Another anxious person may sit quietly in a chair, but his fingernails will be chewed into the quick or he will move his lower jaw slowly from side to side. My point is that tension increases the amount of bodily movement observed in adults.

How much more true that is of an immature child. He doesn't merely drum his fingers on a table when he is anxious; he tries to climb the curtains and walk on the ceiling.

How Early Can the Problem Be Identified?

The severely hyperactive child can be recognized during early toddlerhood. In fact, he can't be ignored. By the time he is thirty months of age he may have exhausted his mother, irritated his siblings, and caused the grandparents to retire from babysitting duties. No family member is "uninvolved" with his problem. Instead of growing out of it, as the physician may promise, he continues to attack his world with the objective of disassembling it. Dr. Domeena Renshaw described one such child in her excellent book *The Hyperactive Child:*

> The youngest patient brought to the author was a 1½-year-old boy, youngest in a sibship of six. The father was a civil engineer. The mother cheerful and sensible. She reported a normal labor but a very rapid delivery. The child developed slowly till age fifteen months when he began to run, not having crawled. He had then begun to speak in sentences, not having babbled at all. From then on, "it was like having a hurricane in the house, everything up for grabs." He would climb out of his crib (by fifteen months) early in the morning and not fall asleep till midnight. Daytime naps had ceased by fifteen months. His activity was ceaseless. He was extremely distractible, never watched TV, never finished a meal without needing to be brought back to his highchair at the table a dozen times. He had no concept of danger, had two greenstick arm fractures from two falls from the same tree (three similar falls resulted in abrasions only). He was considered a "bully" by his sibs and older peers. He did not respond to rewards or punishments.[1]

We will see what happened to this child later in this chapter.

Is There a "Normal" Hyperactivity?

Certainly. Not every child who squirms, churns, and bounces is technically "hyperactive." Most toddlers are "on the move" from dawn to dark (as are their mothers).

Then How Can I Tell Whether My Child Is Just Normally Active or Genuinely Hyperactive? And How Can I Decipher Whether His Problem Is the Result of Emotional or a Physical Impairment?

These questions are difficult to answer, and few parents have the training to resolve them. Your best resource in evaluating your child's problem is your pediatrician or family physician. Even he may have to guess at a diagnosis and its cause. He can, however, make a complete medical evaluation and then refer you, if necessary, to other professionals for specific assistance. Your child may require the services of a remedial reading teacher or a speech and hearing therapist or a psychologist who can assess intellectual and perceptual abilities and offer management advice. You should not try alone to cope with an excessively active child if this additional support and consultation is available.

What Role Does Nutrition Play?

The role of nutrition in hyperactivity is a very controversial issue which I am not qualified to resolve; I can only offer my opinion on the subject. The American people have been told that hyperactivity is a product of red food coloring, too much sugar intake, inadequate vitamins, and many related causes resulting from poor nutrition. I don't doubt for a moment that improper eating habits have the capacity to destroy us physically and could easily be related to the phenomenon of hyperactivity. However, I am of the opinion that the writers of many faddish books on this subject are trying to make their guesses sound like proven facts. Many of the answers are not yet available, which explains why so many "authorities" disagree violently among themselves.

The nutritionists whom I respect most highly are those who take a cautious, scientific approach to these complex questions. I am suspicious of the self-appointed experts who bypass their own professional publications and come directly to the lay public with unsupported conclusions which even their colleagues reject.

The above paragraph may irritate some parents who are following the advice of a lone-wolf nutritional writer. To those readers I can only say, "Do what succeeds." If your child is more calm and sedate when avoiding certain foods, then use your judgment as you continue the successful dietary regimen. Your opinion is probably as valid as mine.

How Common Is Hyperactivity?

Authorities disagree on the incidence of hyperactivity, but this disorder apparently affects between 6 and 10 percent of all children under ten years of age. Males outnumber females four to one.

How Do Parents React?

The mother of a hyperactive child typically experiences a distressing tug of war in her mind. On the one side, she understands her child's problem and feels a deep empathy and love for her little fellow. There is nothing that she wouldn't do to help him. But on the other side, she resents the chaos he has brought into her life. Speedy Gonzales spills his milk and breaks vases and teeters on the brink of disaster throughout the day. He embarrasses his mother in public and shows little appreciation for the sacrifices she is making on his behalf. By the time bedtime arrives, she often feels as if she has spent the entire day in a foxhole.

What happens, then, when genuine love and strong resentment collide in the mind of a mother or father? The inevitable result is parental guilt in sizeable proportions—guilt that is terribly destructive to a woman's peace of mind and even to her health.

What Other Problems Does the Hyperactive Child Face?

The child with exaggerated activity usually experiences three specific difficulties in addition to his frantic motion. First, he is likely to develop psychological problems resulting from rejection by his peers. His nervous energy is not only irritating to adults, but tends to drive away friends as well. He may be branded as a trouble-maker and a goof-off in the classroom. Furthermore, his emotional response is often unstable, swinging unpredictably from laughter to tears in a matter of moments, and causing his peers to think him strange. In short, the hyperactive child can easily fall victim to feelings of inferiority and the emotional upheaval which is inevitably generated by rejection and low self-esteem.

Second, the active child frequently experiences severe learning problems during the school years. He finds it difficult, if not impossible, to remain in his seat and concentrate on his lessons. His attention span is miniscule throughout elementary school, which leads to mischievousness and distractibility while his teachers are speaking. He never seems to know what the educational program is all about, and his frustrated teachers often describe him as being "in a fog."

But there is another academic difficulty which is also extremely common among hyperactive children: visual perceptual problems. A child may have perfectly normal vision, yet not "perceive" symbols and printed material accurately. In other words, his eyes may be perfect but his brain does not process the signal properly. Such a child may "see" letters and numbers reversed or distorted. It is particularly difficult for him to learn to read or write.

Reading is a highly complex neurological skill. It requires the recognition of symbols and their transmittal to the brain, where they must be interpreted, remembered, and (perhaps) spoken as language. Any break in this functional chain will inhibit the final product. Furthermore, this process must occur rapidly enough to permit a steady flow of ideas from the written materials. Many hyperactive children simply do not have the neurological apparatus to develop these skills and are destined to experience failure during the primary grades in school.

What Are the Solutions?

There are dozens of medications which have been shown
to be effective in calming the hyperactive child. Since every
child's chemistry is unique, it may be necessary for a physician to "fish" for the right substance and dosage. Let me
stress that I am opposed to the administration of such drugs
to children who do not require them. In some instances
these substances have been given indiscriminately to children simply because their parents or teachers preferred them
sedated, which is inexcusable. Every medication has an undesirable side effect (even aspirin) and should be administered only after careful evaluation and study. However, if your child displays the symptoms I have described
in the preceding section and has been evaluated by a
neurologist or other knowledgeable physician, you should
not hesitate to accept his prescription of an appropriate
medication. Some dramatic behavioral changes can occur
when the proper substance is identified for a particular
child.

The frantic young patient described earlier by Dr. Renshaw was placed on dextroamphetamine, with the following results:

> By the third day of treatment he was asleep at 8 P.M.
> and eating with the family was possible with only two
> trips away from the table. He is now six years old, do-
> ing exceptionally well in regular first grade, and is be-
> ing seen at the clinic at three-month intervals. (p. 81)

But Won't the Long-term Use of Medication Increase the Possibility of My Child Becoming a Drug User During Adolescence?

Most authorities feel that the use of medication in childhood does not necessarily lead to drug abuse later in life. In fact, a federal task force was appointed in 1971 to consider that possibility. The conclusion from their investigation emphasized the appropriateness of medications in treatment of hyperactive children. Some children need, and should get, the proper calming agent.

Do Medications Solve All the Problems?

Usually not. Let's consider the three primary symptoms as related to medications:

1. *Hyperactivity.* The proper prescription can be very effective in "normalizing" a child's motor activity. Treatment is most successful in controlling this symptom.

2. *Psychological difficulties.* Medication is less effective in eliminating emotional problems. Once a child has been "slowed down," the process of building his self-image and social acceptance must begin in earnest. The administration of drugs may make that objective possible, but it does not, in itself, eradicate the problem.

3. *Visual-perceptual problems.* Drug usage is of no value in resolving neurological malfunctions which interfere with perception. There are training materials available which have been shown to be helpful, including those provided by the Marianne Frostig Center for Educational Therapy. Dr. Frostig is a pioneer in the field of learning disabilities, and has provided books, films, and evaluative tests for use by teachers and trained professionals. Your local school dis-

trict can obtain a list of available resources by contacting this organization at 5981 Venice Boulevard, Los Angeles, California 90034. Many school districts also provide special classes for children with unique learning disabilities, which can be of inestimable value to a handicapped student.

It is obvious that drug therapy cannot provide the total remedy. A pharmaceutical approach must be combined with parental adaptations and educational alternatives, among others.

How Does the Parent "Discipline" a Hyperactive Child?

It is often assumed that an excessively active child should be indulged, simply because he has a physical problem. I couldn't disagree more. Every youngster needs the security of defined limits, and the hyperactive boy or girl is no exception. Such a child should be held responsible for his behavior, like the rest of the family. Of course, your level of expectation must be adjusted to fit his limitations. For example, most children can be required to sit in a chair for disciplinary reasons, whereas the hyperactive child would not be able to remain there. Similarly, spankings are sometimes ineffective with a highly excitable little bundle of electricity. As with every aspect of parenthood, disciplinary measures for the hyperactive child must be suited to his unique characteristics and needs.

How, then, is the child to be controlled? What advice is available for the parents of a child with this problem? Listed below are eighteen helpful suggestions quoted from the previously mentioned text by Dr. Renshaw.[2]

1. Be carefully consistent in rules and disciplines.
2. Keep your own voice quiet and slow. Anger is normal. Anger can be controlled. Anger does not mean you do not love a child.
3. Try hard to keep your emotions cool by bracing for expectable turmoil. Recognize and respond to any positive behavior, however small. If you search for good things, you will find a few.
4. Avoid a ceaselessly negative approach: "Stop"—"Don't" —"No"—
5. Separate behavior which you may not like, from the child's person, which you like, e.g., "I like you. I don't like your tracking mud through the house."
6. Have a very clear routine for this child. Construct a timetable for waking, eating, play, TV, study, chores, and bedtime. Follow it flexibly although he disrupts it. Slowly your structure will reassure him until he develops his own.
7. Demonstrate new or difficult tasks, using action accompanied by short, clear, quiet, explanations. Repeat the demonstration until learned. This uses audio-visual-sensory perceptions to reinforce the learning. The memory traces of a hyperkinetic child take longer to form. Be patient and repeat.
8. Try a separate room or a part of a room which is his own special area. Avoid brilliant colors or complex patterns in decor. Simplicity, solid colors, minimal clutter, and a worktable facing a blank wall away from distractions assist concentration. A hyperkinetic child cannot "filter" out overstimulation himself yet.
9. Do one thing at a time: give him one toy from a closed box; clear the table of everything else when coloring; turn off the radio/TV when he is doing homework. Multiple stimuli prevent his concentration from focusing on his primary task.
10. Give him responsibility, which is essential for growth. The task should be within his capacity, although the assignment may need much supervision. Acceptance and recognition of his efforts (even when imperfect) should not be forgotten.
11. Read his pre-explosive warning signals. Quietly intervene to avoid explosions by distracting him or discussing the conflict calmly. Removal from the battle zone to

the sanctuary of his room for a few minutes is useful.

12. Restrict playmates to one or at most two at one time, because he is so excitable. Your home is more suitable, so you can provide structure and supervision. Explain your rules to the playmate and briefly tell the other parent your reasons.

13. Do not pity, tease, be frightened by, or overindulge this child. He has a special condition of the nervous system which is manageable.

14. Know the name and dose of his medications. Give these regularly. Watch and remember the effects to report back to your physician.

15. Openly discuss any fears you have about the use of medications with your physician.

16. Lock up all medications, including these, to avoid accidental misuse.

17. Always supervise the taking of medication, even if it is routine over a long period of years. Responsibility remains with the parents! One day's supply at a time can be put in a regular place and checked routinely as he becomes older and more self-reliant.

18. Share your successful "helps" with his teacher. The outlined ways to help your hyperkinetic child are as important to him as diet and insulin are to a diabetic child.

How Should the Parent Respond to School Failure?

Let's talk about the child with a learning deficit. What should be the attitude of his parent in response to poor classroom performance? Obviously, tutorial assistance and special instruction should be provided if possible. Beyond that, however, I would *strongly* suggest that academic achievement be de-emphasized at home.

Requiring a visually handicapped child to compete academically is like forcing a polio victim to run the hundred yard dash. Imagine a mother and father standing disapprovingly at the end of the track, berating their crippled child as he hobbles across the finish line in last place.

"Why don't you run faster, son?" his mother asks with obvious displeasure.

"I don't think you really care whether you win or lose," says his embarrassed father.

How can this lad explain, if they don't already understand, that his legs will not carry him as fast as those of his peers? All he knows is that the other sprinters run past him to the cheering of the crowd. But who would expect a crippled child to win a race against healthy peers? No one, simply because his handicap is obvious. Everyone can see it.

Unfortunately, the child with a learning deficit is not so well understood. His academic failure is more difficult to understand and may be attributed to laziness, mischievousness or deliberate defiance. Consequently, he experiences pressures to do the impossible. And one of the most serious threats to emotional health occurs when a child faces demands that he *cannot* satisfy.

Let me restate the preceding viewpoint in its most concise terms: I believe in academic excellence. I want to maximize every ounce of intellectual potential which a child possesses. I don't believe in letting him behave irresponsibly simply because he doesn't choose to work. Without question, there is lasting benefit to be derived from educational discipline.

But, on the other hand, some things in life are more important than academic excellence, and self-esteem is one of them. A child can survive, if he must, without knowing a noun from a verb. But if he doesn't have some measure of self-confidence and personal respect, he won't have a chance in life.

I want to assert my conviction that the child who is unequipped to prosper in the traditional educational setting is *not* inferior to his peers. He possesses the same degree of human worth and dignity as the intellectual young super-star. It is a foolish cultural distortion that causes us to evaluate the worth of children according to the abilities and physical features they may (or may not) possess.

Every child is of equal worth in the sight of God, and that is good enough for me. Thus, if my little boy or girl can't be successful in one environment, we'll just look for another. Any loving parent would do the same.

What Does the Future Hold?

In case you haven't heard, help is on the way. The maturation and glandular changes associated with puberty often calm the hyperactive youngster between twelve and eighteen years of age. This explains why we seldom see adults jumping from the backs of chairs and rolling on the floor. But for harassed parents who spend their days chasing a nonstop toddler around the house, there may be little consolation in knowing that the crisis will last only nine more years.

Note: For parents who want to learn more about children with hyperactivity, I would refer them to Dr. Renshaw's excellent book. While the writing style is somewhat technical, it is certainly readable and contains helpful insights. See note 1 for publication details.

QUESTIONS

Question: What do you think of the phrase "Children should be seen and not heard"?

Answer: That statement reveals a profound ignorance of children and their needs. I can't imagine how any loving adult could raise a vulnerable little boy or girl by that philosophy. Children are like clocks, they must be allowed to run!

Question: My six-year-old son has always been an energetic child with some of the other symptoms you described. He has a short attention span and flits from one activity to another. I took him to his pediatrician who said he was not actually hyperactive, in the medical sense, and should not be given medication for this mild problem. However, he's beginning to have learning problems in school because he can't stay in his seat and concentrate on his lessons. What should I do?

Answer: It is likely that your son is immature in comparison with his peers, and could profit from being retained in the first grade next year. If his birthday is between December 1 and July 1, I would definitely ask the school guidance office to advise you on this possibility. Retaining an immature boy during his early school career (kindergarten or first grade) can give him a great social and academic advantage throughout the remaining years of elementary school. However, it is very important to help him "save face" with his peers. If possible, he should change schools for at least a year to avoid embarrassing questions and ridicule from his former classmates.

Question: He wets the bed, too. Can you offer any advice for dealing with that recurring problem?

Answer: The fact that your child has enuresis (is a bedwetter) is further confirmation that you have a boy who is developmentally immature. Bed-wetting is often part of the pattern you described above. There is no reason to worry about his babyishness. Each child has his own timetable of maturation, and some are in no great hurry. However, enuresis can produce emotional and social distress for the older child. His peers may call him a "midnight sailor" and less complimentary names. Thus, it is wise to help him conquer the problem as soon as possible. I would recommend that you make use of a buzzer device that emits a loud noise when your boy urinates at night. Sears, Roebuck and Co. sells a unit called a Wee Alert, which I have found effective *when used properly* for children four years of age and older.

Bed-wetting occurs in most cases as a result of very sound sleep, which makes it difficult, if not impossible, for the child to learn nighttime control on his own. His mind does not respond to the signal or reflex action that ordinarily awakens a lighter sleeper. Fortunately, that reflex action can be trained or conditioned to awaken even a deep sleeper in most instances.

The Wee Alert system produces a very irritating sound when urination occurs at night. The child has been instructed to awaken one parent (determining which one can create some interesting marital arguments) who must place him in a tub of cool water or splash cold water on his face. Both alternatives are unpleasant, of course, but are essential to success of the program. The child is told that this is *not* a form of punishment for wetting the bed. It is necessary to help him break the habit so he can invite friends to spend the night and he can go to other homes, as well. The cold water awakens the child fully and gives him a reason not to want to repeat the experience. It is a form of aversive conditioning, such as is used to help break the habit of smoking. Later, the relaxation immediately prior to urination is associated with the unpleasantness of the bell and the cold water. When that connection is made, urinary control is mastered.

This procedure may take from four to eight weeks to

conquer bed-wetting, but success can occur much more quickly in some cases. My own son remained dry the third night we used the equipment. As indicated in the Wee Alert instructions, it is unnecessary to restrict liquids, get the child up at night, use punishment, etc. None of these standard procedures communicate with the unconscious mind during periods of deep, dreamy sleep. The Wee Alert system apparently does.

(Please note that I did not invent the Wee Alert system and receive no compensation from Sears for recommending this product. I merely suggest the device because it usually works.)

Question: How do you get children to behave politely and responsibly, especially when they pay no attention to your repeated instructions?

Answer: Kids love games of all sorts, especially if adults will get involved with them. It is often possible to turn a teaching situation into a fun activity which "sensitizes" the entire family to the issue you're trying to teach. If you'll pardon yet another personal example, let me tell you how we taught our children to put their napkins in their laps before eating. We tried reminding them for two or three years, but simply weren't getting through. Then we turned it into a family game.

Now, if one of the Dobsons takes a single bite of food before putting his napkin in his lap, he is required to go to his bedroom and count to twenty-five in a loud voice. This game is highly effective, although it has some definite disadvantages. You can't imagine how foolish Shirley and I feel when we're standing in an empty section of the house, counting to twenty-five while our kids giggle. Ryan, particularly, *never* forgets his napkin and he loves to catch the rest of us in a moment of preoccupation. He will sit perfectly still, looking straight ahead until the first bite of food goes in. Then he wheels toward the offender, points his finger, and says, "Gotcha!!"

For all of those many teaching objectives that involve teaching responsibility (rather than conquering willful defiance), game-playing should be considered as the method of choice.

7 An Evaluation of Parent Effectiveness Training (P.E.T.)

The recommendations offered to this point have clearly reflected my conviction that loving parental authority is healthy for children and their families. This concept has been accepted *prima facie* for thousands of years, but is now being challenged vigorously in some professional circles. In fact, the entire Judeo-Christian heritage relating to family life has been contradicted during the past decade. Consequently, the American people have recently been exposed to some of the most foolish ideas in the history of mankind, including open marriage and the "God is dead" theory and the new morality and unisex, to name a few. But at the top of the list of "dumb thinking" is the notion that children are somehow endangered by the conscientious leadership of their loving parents.

The first book on this subject to get wide publicity was written by the well known educator John Holt. Mr. Holt became famous by authoring *How Children Fail,* which was a runaway best seller. Then in 1974, he produced what I consider to be a literary disaster entitled *Escape from Childhood.* The Los Angeles *Times* reviewed his book as follows:

> In the latest (book), he plainly advocates the overthrow of parental authority in just about every area. He sets forth that children, *age whatever,* should have the right to: experience sex, drink and use drugs, drive, vote, work, own property, travel, have a guaranteed income, choose their guardians, control their learning, and have legal and financial responsibility.
>
> In short, Holt is proposing that parents discard the protectorate position they have held over their children in this and other countries over the past several hundred years and thrust them, or rather let them thrust themselves—when they feel like they want to—into the real-life world.[1]

Does that sound foolish to anyone but me? Can you imagine a six-year-old girl driving her own car to an escrow office, where she and her preschool male friend will discuss the purchase of a new home over a martini or two? Can you visualize a teary-eyed mother and father standing in the doorway, saying "goodbye" to their five-year-old son who had decided to pack his teddy bear and go live with someone else? Have we gone completely mad? Discard the protectorate position, indeed!

Let me repeat that these recommendations were not written by an unknown crank from somewhere out in never-

never land. They are the philosophical offerings of one of America's best known educators. And what may be more startling is the reaction Mr. Holt has received to many of his revolutionary ideas. The *Times* quoted him directly in regard to that public response:

> "Oddly enough, the chapter on the matter of drinking and drugs, letting young people do whatever older people do, as well as manage their own sex lives, hasn't brought as much flak as I would have expected . . . The understanding, sympathetic responses (from readers) have clearly outweighed the negative or hostile ones," he said.[2]

John Holt's views are shared by others who "advocate the overthrow of parental authority in just about every area." A psychologist named Richard Farson has written a similar and equally outrageous book entitled *Birthrights: A Bill of Rights for Children*. These men are at the forefront of a movement which the Los Angeles *Times* called, "The Mounting March for Children's Rights." Their writings have inspired an aggressive campaign in Washington and in various state legislatures to implement the objectives of this vigorous movement.

A more reasonable (and less extreme) example of this antiauthority philosophy is incorporated into a program entitled Parent Effectiveness Training. Its creator, Dr. Thomas Gordon, is perhaps the most influential advisor of parents in America today. There are more than 8000 P.E.T. classes in operation throughout the country, each marketing Dr. Gordon's parenting techniques with missionary zeal. More than a quarter of a million parents have taken his course, prompting the New York *Times* to call it "a national movement." Furthermore, many Christians have participated in

168   *The Strong-willed Child*

the P.E.T. courses, and some churches have sponsored the training sessions for their laymen.

In view of the impact of Dr. Gordon's program, it might be helpful to examine his philosophy and recommendations in the light of traditional Christian values.

No Win, No Lose

The most effective aspect of the P.E.T. program involves the teaching of listening skills. Dr. Gordon accurately recognizes the failure of many parents to comprehend what their children are actually saying. They hear the words, of course, but do not discern the true meaning which the child is conveying. The ability to engage in active listening, as it is called, is a valuable skill which should be learned by every parent. I can enthusiastically recommend this feature of Gordon's program.

The essence of the P.E.T. philosophy, however, is expressed in a "no-win—no-lose" approach to parent-child relationships. According to this system, solutions are sought to conflicts which are acceptable to both parties. Let me explain by paraphrasing an example from Gordon's writings which describes a five-year-old girl named Bonnie who doesn't like to get dressed in the morning. Even when her mother awakens her sufficiently early, the kindergartner dawdles and plays, eventually making the family late for its various activities. Mother could yell at Bonnie or she could punish the child for being late or reward her for being on time. Instead, however, Mother discusses the problem with Bonnie, seeking a solution upon which they can mutually agree. During the conversation Bonnie reveals that she doesn't like school anyway, and she would "rather stay home and play with Mommie." Eventually, Mother and

Bonnie agree that if the youngster will hurry each morning, the two of them will spend a fun-filled hour together after school instead of Bonnie's taking her usual nap. In this manner, they developed a plan of action which theoretically resulted in the child's hurrying to get dressed each morning (which Mom wanted) and a fun-and-games session each afternoon, (which Bonnie coveted). Therefore, neither party "won" at the expense of the other, nor did they really "lose."

I would certainly agree that on many occasions compromise and negotiation are appropriate between parent and child. Six-year-old Johnny may voluntarily rest or nap in the afternoon so that he can watch a late evening children's program on television. Mom may offer to drive her ten-year-old son to baseball practice, provided he agrees to keep his room clean and neat. Obviously, there is time and place for negotiation in human affairs, whether it be between father and son, husband and wife, or Henry Kissinger and the Arabs. And when it occurs, the objective is a "no-win—no-lose" consequence for each negotiator.

My concern about P.E.T., then, is not in its use of the conference table when the situation warrants. Rather, it is Gordon's rejection of parental authority in any form. Consider the following quotations from his book:

> The stubborn persistence of the idea that parents must and should use authority in dealing with children has, in my opinion, prevented for centuries any significant change or improvement in the way children are raised by parents and treated by adults. (p. 164)

> Children resent those who have power over them. (p. 177) . . . children do not want the parent to try to limit or modify their behavior by using or

> threatening to use their authority. In short, children want to limit their behavior *themselves,* if it becomes apparent *to them* that their behavior must be limited or modified. Children, like adults, prefer to be their own authority over their behavior. (p. 188)

> My own conviction is that as more people begin to understand power and authority more completely and accept its use as unethical, more parents . . . will be forced to search for creative new non-power methods that all adults can use with children and youth. (p. 191)[3]

These condemnations of authority are also apparent in the books Gordon personally recommends. Two of the authors represented in his "Suggested Reading for Parents" are John Holt and Richard Farson, mentioned earlier. Of Farson's *Birthrights,* Gordon wrote, "This book will help parents construct a new way of looking at their role that frees them from the guilt of total responsibility for their children's values and behavior."

It is my belief that these antiauthority views are directly contradictory to the teachings of Scripture. As mentioned earlier, 1 Timothy 3:4, 5 states, "He [speaking of the father] must have the proper *authority* in his own household, and be able to control and command the respect of his children" (Phillips). Colossians 3:20 expresses this divine principle to the younger generation, "Children, obey your parents in all things, for this is well pleasing unto the Lord" (KJV). I find no place in the Bible where our little ones are installed as co-discussants at a conference table, deciding what they will and will not accept from the older generation.

Why is parental authority so vigorously supported throughout the Bible? Is it simply catering to the whims of oppressive, power-hungry adults, as Gordon would surmise? No, the leadership of parents plays a significant role in the development of a child! By learning to yield to the loving authority (leadership) of his parents, a child learns to submit to other forms of authority which will confront him later in life. The way he sees his parents' leadership sets the tone for his eventual relationships with his teachers, school principal, police, neighbors, and employers. Despite P.E.T.'s disregard for these forms of authority, they are necessary to healthy human relationships. Without respect for leadership, there is anarchy, chaos, and confusion for everyone concerned.

There is an even more important reason for the preservation of authority in the home: while yielding to the loving leadership of their parents, children are also learning to yield to the benevolent leadership of God Himself. It is a well known fact that a child identifies his parents with God, whether the adults want that role or not. Most children "see" God the way they perceive their earthly fathers (and, to a lesser degree, their mothers). This fact was illustrated in our home when little Ryan was just two years old. Since the time of his babyhood, he had seen his sister, mother, and father say "grace" before eating our meals, for we always thank God for our food in that way. But because of his age, the little toddler had never been asked to lead the prayer. On one occasion when I was gone, Shirley put the lunch on the table and spontaneously turned to Ryan saying, "Would you like to pray for our food, today?" Her unexpected request apparently startled him and he glanced around nervously, then clasped his little hands together and said, "I love you, Daddy. Amen."

When I returned home and heard about Ryan's prayer,

it was immediately apparent that my son had actually confused me with God. And I'll confess, I wish he hadn't! I appreciated the thought, but I was uncomfortable with its implications. It's too big a job for an ordinary dad to handle. There will be times when I will disappoint my son —times when I will be too tired to be what he needs of me—times when my human frailties will be all too apparent. There have already been occasions when I have fallen short of his expectation, and the older he gets, the greater will be the gap between who I am and who he thought I was. No, I don't want to represent God to my son and daughter. But whether I like it or not, they have given me this position, and your children have done the same to you! The Creator has given to us parents the awesome responsibility of representing Him to our children. As such, we must reflect the two aspects of Divine nature to the next generation. First, our Heavenly Father is a God of unlimited love, and our children must become acquainted with His mercy and tenderness through our own love toward them. But make no mistake about it, our Lord is also the possessor of majestic authority! The universe is ordered by a supreme Lord who requires obedience from His children and has warned them that "the wages of sin is death." To show our little ones love without authority is as serious a distortion of God's nature as to reveal an iron-fisted authority without love.

From this perspective, then, it is unreasonable to think that a child who has only "negotiated" with his parents and teachers has been learning to submit to the authority of the Almighty. And I find this fact to be absolutely irrefutable; if a little child is taught to disrespect the authority of his parents, systematically from the tender years of childhood —to mock their leadership, to "sass" them and disobey their instructions, to exercise extreme self-will from the earliest moments of awareness—then it is most unlikely that this same child will turn his face up to God, about twenty years later, and say humbly, "Here am I, Lord; send me!" To repeat, a child learns to yield to the authority of God by first learning to submit (rather than bargain) to the leadership of his parents. And the literal application of P.E.T. sacrifices that experience!

But what does the apostle Paul mean in the letter to Timothy when he sanctions the "proper authority?" Does he give parents the right to be mean and harsh with their children, disregarding their feelings and instilling fearful anxiety? Certainly not! Let me refer again to Ephesians 6:4 which spells out the approach: "And now a word to you parents. Don't keep on scolding and nagging your children, making them angry and resentful. Rather, bring them up with the loving discipline the Lord himself approves, with suggestions and godly advice" (TLB). Whereas Gordon and his allies write derogatorily about the uses of parental "power," the Bible strongly and consistently supports the role of loving, parental *leadership* in raising a child. Forced to choose between two alternatives, I'll cast my lot with the immutable, everlasting Word of God!

Not only is Gordon's view of authority of concern to me but I am also bothered by two other aspects of his philosophy which are widely echoed in non-Christian circles:

1. *"Children Are Basically 'Good,' But They Are Corrupted by Bad Relationships with Parents and Others in Their Society."*

Gordon expressed this optimistic concept when appearing on Mike Douglas's television show in January, 1976.

He also revealed that perspective throughout his book. Concerning the tendency to lie, for example, he wrote:

> While children lie a lot because so many parents rely heavily on rewards and punishment, I firmly believe that the tendency to lie is not natural in youngsters. It is a learned response. . .[4]

I wish that Gordon's assessment of human nature were accurate. But again, it contradicts Scriptural understandings. Jeremiah wrote, "The heart is deceitful above all things, and desperately wicked: who can know it?" (Jer. 17:9 KJV). Jeremiah's inspired insight into human nature is validated by the sordid history of mankind. The record of civilization is blotted by murder, war, rape, and plundering from the time of Adam forward. Surely, during those thousands of years, there must have been at least *one* generation for whom parents did things right. Yet greed, lust, and selfishness have characterized us all. Is this nature also evident in children? King David thought so, for he confessed, ". . . in sin did my mother conceive me" (Ps. 51:5 KJV).

What meaningful difference, then, is made by the distinction between the two views of children? Practically everything, in fact. Parents who believe all toddlers are infused with goodness and sunshine are urged to get out of the way and let their pleasant nature unfold. On the other hand, parents who recognize the inevitable internal war between good and evil will do their best to influence the child's choices—to shape his will and provide a solid spiritual foundation. They recognize the dangers of willful defiance as expressed in 1 Samuel 15:23—"For rebellion is as bad as the sin of witchcraft, and stubbornness is as bad as worshiping idols." (TLB)

My entire book, you see, is a product of the biblical orientation to human nature. We are not typically kind and loving and generous and yielded to God. Our tendency is toward selfishness and stubbornness and sin. We are all, in effect, "strong-willed children" as we stand before God. Jesus, who represents the only sinless human being, expressed the opposite nature when He said in the Garden of Gethsemane, "Not my will but Thine be done." Thus, the Christian parent hopes to lead his child to this Jesus Christ, who alone can "cleanse" him of rebellion. It's a very old explanation of human nature and it sounds terribly unscientific. But the Bible teaches it, and I believe it. That leads us to the second area of concern in Gordon's writings.

2. *"We Have No Rights or Obligation As Parents to Instill Our Values, Attitudes, and Beliefs in Our Children."*

This foolish notion would have brought universal scorn and contempt if uttered a few years ago, yet Gordon assaults the wisdom of the ages without a flinch. He wrote in P.E.T.,

> The problem is *who is to decide* what is in the best interest of society. The child? The parent? Who knows best? These are difficult questions, and there are dangers in leaving the determination of "best interest" with the parent. He may not be wise enough to make this determination.[5]

I sympathize with Dr. Gordon in his suspiciousness of human wisdom. I would lack confidence, too, if I had no standard or guide upon which to base my parental judgments and determinations. However, the Christian mother and father need not "lean on their own understanding," for they have access to the wisdom of God Himself. The Creator of heaven and earth and little children has shared His knowledge with us in the form of eternal truths. Furthermore, he inspired Solomon to write the book of Proverbs in which we are urged to "train up a child in the way he should go: and when he is old, he will not depart from it."

It is apparent to me as I consider the fundamentals of Parent Effectiveness Training that Tom Gordon does not draw his precepts and inspiration from the same interpretation of biblical principles on which I depend. In fact, I'm inclined to see his system as only one of many recent offerings in the field of psychology which blatantly contradict the Judeo-Christian ethic. Traditions which have been honored for several thousand years are suddenly vilified. Not even the flag, motherhood, and apple pie are safe; we burned the flag in the sixties, we are mocking motherhood in the seventies, and the way I've got it figured, apple pie is living on borrowed time!

A Final Comment

Portions of the preceding discussion were first published by the editors of *Moody Monthly,*[6] who asked me to write this article. Having considered my earlier views, however, I may have underemphasized the beneficial aspects of the P.E.T. classes. No successful program is completely devoid of useful information, and it would be unfair to mention only P.E.T.'s shortcomings. These sessions offer some worthwhile suggestions in the area of listening skills, in the use of parent-child negotiation, and in the cultivation of parental tolerance. Furthermore, there are few alternatives available for parents who seek to understand their children and keep them healthy.

Nevertheless, it is my view that the great flaws in Tom Gordon's philosophy far outweigh the benefits. They are, again: (1) his failure to understand the proper role of authority in the home; (2) his humanistic viewpoint which teaches that children are born innately "good," and then learn to do wrong; (3) his tendency to weaken parental resolve to *instill* spiritual principles systematically during a child's "teachable" years. All things considered, therefore, I would not recommend that Christian parents attend the P.E.T. program unless they are braced for the contradictions and deficiencies I have outlined.

QUESTIONS

Question: Dr. Gordon often cites an illustration of a child who puts his feet on an expensive item of living room furniture. His parents become irritated at this gesture and order him to take his dirty shoes from the chair or table. Gordon then shows how much more politely those parents would have handled the same indiscretion if the offender had been an adult guest. They might have cautiously asked him to remove his shoes, but would certainly not have felt it necessary to discipline or criticize the visitor. Dr. Gordon then asks, "Aren't children people, too? Why don't we treat them with the same respect that we do our adult friends?" Would you comment on this example?

Answer: I have heard Dr. Gordon relate the same illustration and feel that it contains both truth and distortion. If his point is that we need to exercise greater kindness and respect in dealing with our children, then I certainly agree. However, to equate children with adult visitors in the home is an error in reasoning. I do not bear *any* responsibility for teaching proper manners and courtesy to my guests; I certainly do have that obligation on behalf of my children. Furthermore, the illustration implies that children and adults think and act identically, and have the same needs. They don't. As described previously, a child often behaves offensively for the precise purpose of testing the courage of his parents. He wants them to establish firm boundaries. By contrast, a guest who puts his feet on a coffee table is more likely to be acting through ignorance or insensitivity.

More important, this illustration cleverly redefines the traditional parental relationship with children. Instead of bearing direct responsibility for training and teaching and leading them, Mom and Dad have become cautious co-equals who can only hope their independent little "guests" will gradually get the message.

No, our children are not casual guests in our home. They have been loaned to us temporarily for the purpose of loving them and instilling a foundation of values on which their future lives will be built. And we will be accountable through eternity for the way we discharge that responsibility.

Question: You referred to the "proper" use of authority as opposed to raw parental power. Dr. Gordon uses these concepts interchangeably throughout his book. Is there a distinction, and if so, what is it?

Answer: You are right in saying that Tom Gordon uses these terms synonymously in Parent Effectiveness Training. Consider the following quotations to that effect:

1. Probably the most frequent attitude about *power and authority* expressed by parents in the P.E.T. classes is that it (a singular pronoun referring to a singular subject) is justified because of parents' responsibility . . . (p. 190)
2. My own conviction is that as more people begin to

understand *power and authority* more completely and accept its use (singular pronoun and verb) as unethical . . . (p. 191)

3. Children do not want the parent to try to limit or modify their behavior by using or threatening to use *authority*. [He did not say power; he was opposing the use of authority, which he perceives as synonymous with power.] (p. 188)

4. [NOTE THIS ONE:] The use of parental *authority* (or *power*), seemingly effective under certain conditions, is quite ineffective under other conditions. [THE PARENTHESES ARE HIS, NOT MINE.] (p. 169)[7]

There are at least twenty other references in which Dr. Gordon blurs the distinction between power and authority. I can only assume that he views all authority as a form of unethical oppression. In fact, he stated that viewpoint very plainly in the second quotation, above.

In my opinion, the two concepts are as different as love and hate. Parental power can be defined as a hostile form of manipulation in order to satisfy selfish adult purposes. As such, it disregards the best interests of the little child on whom it tramples, and produces a relationship of fear and intimidation. Drill instructors in the Marine Corps have been known to depend on this form of power to indoctrinate their beleaguered recruits.

Proper authority, by contrast, is defined as loving *leadership*. Without decision-makers and others who agree to follow, there is inevitable chaos and confusion and disorder in human relationships. Loving authority is the glue that holds social orders together, and it is absolutely necessary for the healthy functioning of a family.

There are times when I say to my child, "Ryan, you are tired because you were up too late last night. I want you to brush your teeth right now and put on your pajamas." My words may sound like a suggestion, but Ryan would be wise to remember who's making it. If that is parental power, according to Dr. Gordon's definition, then so be it. I do not always have time to negotiate, nor do I feel obligated in every instance to struggle for compromises. I have the *authority* to do what I think is in Ryan's best interest, and there are times when I expect him not to negotiate, but to *obey.* And as I said, his learning to yield to my loving leadership is excellent training for his later submission to the loving authority of God. This is very different from the use of vicious and hostile power, resulting from the fact that I outweigh him.

Question: How about Gordon's suggested use of "I" messages, versus "you" messages?

Answer: There is substantial truth in the basic idea. "I" messages can request change or improvement without being offensive: "Diane, it embarrasses me when our neighbors see your messy room. I wish you would straighten it." By contrast, "You" messages often attack the personhood of the recipient and put him on the defensive: "Why don't you keep your stuff picked up?! So help me, Diane, you get sloppier and more irresponsible every day." I agree with Dr. Gordon that the first method of communicating is usually superior to the second, and there is wisdom in his recommendation.

However, let's suppose I have taken my four-year-old son, Dale, to the market where he breaks all known rules. He throws a temper tantrum because I won't buy him a balloon, and he hits the daughter of another customer, and grabs a handful of gum at the checkout stand. When I get darlin' Dale outside the store there is little doubt that he is going to hear a few "you" messages—such as, "When *you* get home, young man, *you* are going to have *your* bottom tanned!"

From my perspective, again, there are a few occasions in the life of a parent when he speaks not as an equal or a comrade or a pal, but as an *authority*. And in those circumstances, an occasional "you" message will fit the circumstance better than an expression of personal frustration by the parent.

Question: Dr. Gordon said parents cannot know what is in the best interest of their children. Do you claim to make weighty decisions on behalf of your kids with unshakable confidence? How do you know that what you're doing will ultimately be healthy for them?

Answer: It is certain that I will make mistakes and errors. My human frailties are impossible to hide and my children occasionally fall victim to those imperfections. But I cannot abandon my responsibilities to provide leadership, simply because I lack infinite wisdom and insight. Besides, I do have more experience and a better perspective on which to base those decisions than my children possess at this time. I've been where they're going.

Perhaps a crude example would be illustrative. My daughter has a pet hamster (uncreatively named Hammy) who has a passion for freedom. He spends a portion of every night gnawing on the metal bars of his cage and forcing his head through the trap door. Recently I sat watching Hammy busily trying to escape. But I was not the only one observing the furry little creature. Sitting in the shadows a few feet away was old Sigmund, our dachshund. His erect ears, squinted eyes, and panting tongue betrayed his sinister thoughts. Siggie was thinking, "Come on baby, break through to freedom! Bite those bars, Hambone, and I'll give you a thrill like you've never experienced!"

How interesting, I thought, that the hamster's greatest desire would bring him instant and violent death if he should be so unfortunate to achieve it. Hammy simply lacked the perspective to realize the folly of his wishes. The application to human experience was too striking to be missed and I shook my head silently as the animal drama spoke to me. There are occasions when the longings and desires of our children would be harmful or disastrous if granted. They would choose midnight bedtime hours and no schoolwork and endless cartoons on television and chocolate sundaes by the dozen. And in later years, they might not see the harm of drug abuse and premarital sex and a life of uninterrupted fun and games. Like Hammy, they lack the "perspective" to observe the dangers which lurk in the shadows. Alas, many young people are "devoured" before they even know that they have made a fatal mistake.

Then my thoughts meandered a bit farther to my own relationship with God and the requests I submit to Him in personal prayer. I wondered how many times I had asked Him to open the door on my "cage," not appreciating the security it was providing. I resolved to accept His negative answers with greater submission in the future.

Returning to the question, let me repeat that my decisions on behalf of my children do not reflect infinite wisdom. They do, however, emanate from love and an intense desire to do the best I can. Beyond that, the ultimate outcome is committed to God virtually every day of my life.

Question: You implied earlier that children find it difficult to accept love before they have tested the courage and strength of their leaders. Why do you think this is true?

Answer: I don't know. But every school teacher will verify the fact that respect for authority must *precede* the acceptance of love. Those teachers who try to spread love in

September and discipline next January are destined for trouble. It won't work. (That's why I recommended—half seriously—that teachers not smile 'til Thanksgiving!)

Perhaps the most frustrating experience of my professional career occurred when I was asked to speak to a group of college students who were majoring in education. Most of these men and women were in their final year of preparation, and would soon be teaching in their own classrooms. The distress that I felt came from my inability to convince these idealistic young people of the principle described above. They really believed that they could pour out love and gain instant respect from these rebels who had been at war with everyone. I felt empathy for the new teachers who would soon find themselves in the jungles of inner city schools, alone and afraid. They were bound to get their "love" thrown back in their startled faces. *Students simply cannot accept a teacher's love until they know that the giver is worthy of their respect.*

It should come as no shock to the reader by this point that I believe in the value of authority in the classroom, as well as in the home. In its absence, we have the situation where teachers are afraid of the principal, the principal is afraid of the superintendent, the superintendent is afraid of the school board, the school board is afraid of the parents, the parents are afraid of the kids, and, would you believe, the kids aren't afraid of anybody!

Though I am technically unqualified to extend this principle into the area of theology, I will share my personal views. It is my deep conviction that man's relationship with God is a reflection of the same phenomenon.

We had to understand the scope of His majesty and authority—and even His wrath—before we could comprehend the depth of His love expressed through the life and death of Jesus! Thus, it is logical that He gave us the content of the Old Testament before the New.

Few things concern me more as a Christian layman than for ministers to focus on one of these divine messages of love and justice to the exclusion of the other. Those who concentrate *only* on judgment and wrath are presenting an image of God that is distorted. He is also a God of infinite love. But the more common distortion in this permissive day is to go to the opposite extreme, depicting God as a doting grandfather who winks at sin and ignores the disobedience of His children. Nowhere in the Bible is this description found.

Though it seems contradictory, those ministers who focus only on the love of God make it impossible for their listeners to comprehend that love. You see, without an understanding of the justice of our Creator and of our obligations to serve Him—and of His promise to punish wickedness—Jesus' death on the cross is of no consequence. He died to provide a remedy for the curse of sin! Unless one understands the curse—the disease—then there is no need for a cure.

Similarly, penicillin is nothing more than a sticky, gooey substance until we understand the meaning of bacterial infection. It is only when one comprehends the way bacteria can destroy the human body that antibiotics assume the significance of "miracle cures." It seems to me that many ministers have told their congregations that Jesus loves them, but deprived them of any true understanding of His most miraculous redemptive gift.

Thus, I feel that the ministers who "edit out" the unpopular themes of the Bible are doing a great disservice to their congregations and may even be yielding to cowardice. Someone wrote, "Silence is not always golden; sometimes it's just yellow." I'm inclined to agree.

Question: Would you comment on methods of discipline that are typical in various churches. Our program tends to be rather wild, and we need to tighten it down. What would you suggest?

Answer: You have touched one of my "sensitive nerves." Perhaps I can best reply by quoting from the manuscript of a recent family life seminar in which the comments of several participants were recorded word for word by a court reporter.[8]

Rev. Dobson: I have heard you express some criticism of the Christian church generally with regard to discipline and behavior in Sunday schools. It ought to be restated here.

Dr. Dobson: Well, it has been my strong conviction that the church should support the family in its attempt to implement biblical principles in the home. This is especially true with reference to the teaching of respect for authority. This isn't an easy time to be a parent because authority has eroded drastically in our society. Therefore, mothers and fathers who are trying to teach respect and responsibility to their children, as the Bible prescribes, need all the help they can get, particularly from the church.

But in my opinion, the church fails miserably at this point. There is no aspect of the church mission that I feel is weaker or more ineffective than discipline in the Sunday school. Parents who have struggled to maintain order and respect all week send their kids off to church on Sunday morning and what happens? They are permitted to throw erasers and shoot paper wads and swing on the light fixtures. This is particularly distressing to me. I am not referring to one denomination. I've seen it happen in almost all of them. In fact, I think I was one of those eraser throwers in my day.

Rev. Dobson: Why do you think our Sunday schools are so lax and permissive?

Dr. Dobson: Teachers are volunteers who may not know how to handle kids. But more important, they are afraid of irritating sensitive parents. They don't feel they have a right to teach children to respect God's house. If they try, they might anger Mama Bear and lose the entire family.

Dr. Cunningham: And they well could. That's the problem. People are so sensitive about their kids. I came through a permissive atmosphere in the Chicago public school system where a teacher was forbidden by law to touch a child— and the same restriction was put on the police department. I've seen kids in that city just stand and taunt policemen and dare them to do anything to them by threatening to sue. Everybody is so scared of lawsuits, you know, and is afraid to reprimand or punish someone else's child.

Dr. Dobson: I'm not recommending that we spank children in the Sunday school, of course. But there are ways to maintain order among children, once we decide that it is important to us. Training sessions can help teachers to do a better job. Pastors can back up Sunday school workers, etc. My concern is that we can't seem to agree that discipline has a place on Sunday morning. In its absence, the chaos that results is an insult to God and to the meaning of worship. You can't accomplish anything in an atmosphere of confusion. You can't teach students when they don't even hear you.

Dr. Cunningham: I couldn't agree with you more. We are trying to insist on discipline and obedience in our church Sunday program. I don't think we have to lose families by doing so. We are just obligated to deal with some children in more creative, meaningful ways—just like they have to do in the public school. We may remove a child from the setting or perhaps have a teacher assigned to him alone until he cools down. I would not want to say, "You can't come back to Sunday school," to any child. Instead, we will try to adapt. We will say, "We care so much about this child that we're going to go to whatever lengths are necessary to try to communicate God's Word to him. And so, parents, we wanted you to know how we are having to approach instruction of your child. We hope we have your support. We love this child and we care about him and we want him to make it. So when this kind of experience is no longer necessary, we'll reintroduce him to the classroom."

Dr. Dobson: I like that, Paul.

8 The Strong-willed Adolescent

(Is there any Other Kind?)

Alas, we arrive now at the door of adolescence: that dynamic time of life which comes in with a pimple and goes out with a beard—those flirtatious years when girls begin to powder and boys begin to puff. It's an exciting phase of childhood, I suppose, but to be honest, I wouldn't want to stumble through it again. I doubt that the reader would either. We adults remember all too clearly the fears and jeers and tears that represented our own tumultuous youth. Perhaps that is why parents begin to quake and tremble when their children approach the adolescent years. (By the way, have you heard of the new wristwatch created ex-

189

clusively for the anxious parents of teen-agers? After 11 P.M. it wrings its hands every fifteen minutes.)

It would be a great mistake to imply that I have immediate answers to every problem faced by the perplexed parents of adolescents. I recognize my own limitations and willingly admit that it is often easier to write about teen-age turmoil than it is to cope with it in real life. Whenever I'm tempted to become self-important and authoritative on this or any other subject, I'm reminded of what the mother whale told her baby: "When you get to the top and start to 'blow,' that's when you get harpooned!" With that admonition in mind, let me humbly offer several suggestions which may be helpful in coping with the strong-willed adolescent.

1. A Teen-ager Is Often Desperately in Need of Respect and Dignity. Give Him These Gifts!

The period of *early* adolescence is typically a painful time of life, marked by rapid physical and emotional changes. This characteristic difficulty was expressed by a seventh-grade boy who had been asked to recite Patrick Henry's historic speech at a Bicentennial program in 1976. But when the young man stood nervously before an audience of parents, he became confused and blurted out, "Give me puberty or give me death!" His statement is not as ridiculous as it sounds. Many teens sincerely believe they must choose between those dubious alternatives.

The thirteenth and fourteenth years commonly are the most difficult twenty-four months in life. It is during this time that self-doubt and feelings of inferiority reach an all-time high, amidst the greatest social pressures yet experienced. An adolescent's worth as a human being hangs precariously on peer group acceptance, which is notoriously fickle. Thus, relatively minor evidences of rejection or ridicule are of major significance to those who already see themselves as fools and failures. It is difficult to overestimate the impact of having no one to sit with on the school-sponsored bus trip, or of not being invited to an important event, or of being laughed at by the "in" group, or of waking up in the morning to find seven shiny new pimples on your bumpy forehead, or of being slapped by the girl you thought had liked you as much as you liked her. Some boys and girls consistently face this kind of social catastrophe throughout their teen years. They will never forget the experience.

The self-esteem of an early adolescent is also assaulted in the Western culture by his youthful status. All of the highly advertised adult privileges and vices are forbidden to him because he is "too young." He can't drive or marry or enlist or drink or smoke or work or leave home. And his sexual desires are denied gratification at a time when they scream for release. The only thing he is permitted to do, it seems, is stay in school and read his dreary textbooks. This is an overstatement, of course, but it is expressed from the viewpoint of the young man or woman who feels disenfranchised and insulted by society. Much of the anger of today's youth is generated by their perception of this "injustice."

Dr. Urie Bronfenbrenner, eminent authority on child development at Cornell University, has also identified the period of early adolescence as the most destructive years of life. He expressed these concerns in a taped interview with Susan Byrne, subsequently published in *Psychology Today*, May 1977.

In that article, Bronfenbrenner recalled being asked

during a U.S. Senate hearing to indicate the most critical years in a child's development. He knew that the Senators expected him to emphasize the importance of preschool experience, reflecting the popular notion that all significant learning takes place during the first six years of life. However, Bronfenbrenner said he had never been able to validate that assumption. He agreed that the preschool years are vital, but so is every other phase of childhood. In fact, he told the Senate committee that the junior high years are probably the most critical to the development of a child's mental health. It is during this period of self-doubt that the personality is often assaulted and damaged beyond repair. Consequently, said Bronfenbrenner, it is not unusual for healthy, happy children to enter junior high school, but then emerge two years later as broken, discouraged teen-agers.

I couldn't agree more emphatically with Bronfenbrenner's opinion at this point. Junior high school students are typically brutal to one another, attacking and slashing a weak victim in much the same way a pack of northern wolves kill and devour a deformed carabao. Few events stir my righteous indignation more than seeing a vulnerable child—fresh from the hand of the Creator in the morning of his life—being taught to hate himself and despise his physical body and wish he had never been born. I am determined to give my assistance to those boys and girls who desperately need a friend during this period of intensive self-doubt.

Not only do I remember the emotional conflicts of my own early adolescence, but I have had ample opportunity since then to observe this troubled time of life in others. I was privileged to teach in public schools from 1960 to 1963, and two of those profitable years were spent at the junior high level. I taught science and math to 225 rambunctious troops each day, although I learned much more from them than they did from me. There on the firing line is where my concepts of discipline began to solidify. The workable solutions were validated and took their place in a system I know to be practical. But the lofty theories dreamed up by grandmotherly educators exploded like so much TNT when tested on the battlefield each day.

One of the most important lessons of those years related to the matter of low self-esteem, which we have been discussing. It became clear to me very early that I could impose all manner of discipline and strict behavioral requirements on my students, *provided* I treated each young person with genuine dignity and respect. I earned their friendship before and after school, during lunch, and through classroom encounters. I was tough, especially when challenged, but never discourteous, mean, or insulting. I defended the underdog and tenaciously tried to build each child's confidence and self-respect. However, I never compromised my standards of deportment. Students entered my classroom without talking each day. They did not chew gum, or behave disrespectfully, or curse or stab one another with ball point pens. I was clearly the captain of the ship and I directed it with military zeal.

The result of this combination of kindness and firm discipline stands as one of the most pleasant memories of my professional life. I *loved* my students and had every reason to believe that I was loved in return. I actually missed them on weekends (a fact my wife never quite understood). At the end of the final year when I was packing my books and saying goodbye, there were twenty-five or thirty teary-eyed kids who hung around my gloomy room for several hours and finally stood sobbing in the parking lot as I drove away. And yes, I shed a few tears of my own that day. (Please forgive this self-congratulatory paragraph. I haven't bothered to tell you about my failures, which are far less interesting.)

One young lady to whom I said "goodbye" in the school parking lot in 1963 called me on the telephone during 1975. I hadn't seen Julie for more than a decade, and she had become a grown woman in the ensuing years. I remembered her as a seventh-grader whose crisis of confidence was revealed in her sad brown eyes. She seemed embarrassed by her Latin heritage and the fact that she was slightly overweight. She had only one friend, who moved away the following year.

Julie and I talked amiably on the phone about old times at Cedarlane Junior High School, and then she asked me a pointed question: "Where do you go to church?"

I told her where we attended, and she replied, "I wonder if you'd mind my visiting there some Sunday morning?"

I said, "Julie, I'd be delighted."

The next week, my wife and I met Julie in the vestibule of the sanctuary, and she sat with us during the service. Through a process of growth and guidance in subsequent months, this young woman became a vibrant Christian. She now participates in the choir, and many members of the congregation have commented on the radiant glow she seems to transmit when singing.

I stopped her as we were leaving the church a few months later and said, "Julie, I want to ask you a question. Will you tell me why you went to so much trouble to obtain my unlisted phone number and call me last fall. Why did you want to talk to me after all those years, and why did you ask what church I attended?"

Julie thought for a moment and then paid me the highest compliment anyone has ever sent my way. She said, "Because when I was a seventh-grade student in junior high school, you were the *only* person in my life who acted like you respected and believed in me . . . and I wanted to know your God."

If you can communicate that kind of dignity to your oppressed and harassed teen-agers, then many of the characteristic discipline problems of adolescence can be circumvented. That is, after all, the best way to deal with people of *any* age.

Let's look now at the second suggestion which can be, in effect, a means of implementing the first.

2. Verbalize Conflicts and Re-establish the Boundaries

There is often an *irrationality* associated with adolescence which can be terribly frustrating to parents. Let me offer an illustration which may explain the problem.

A student graduated from medical school in Los Angeles a few years ago and was required as part of his internship to spend a few weeks working in a psychiatric hospital. However, he was given little orientation to the nature of mental illness and he mistakenly thought he could "reason" his patients back to a world of reality. One schizophrenic inmate was particularly interesting to him, because the man believed himself to be dead.

"Yeah, it's true," the patient would tell anyone who asked. "I'm dead. Been dead for years."

The intern couldn't resist trying to "talk" the schizophrenic out of his fantasy. Therefore, he sat down with the patient and said, "I understand you think you're dead. Is that right?"

"Sure is," replied the inmate. "I'm deader than a doornail."

The intern continued, "Well, tell me this, do dead people bleed?"

"No, of course not," answered the schizophrenic, sounding perfectly sane. The intern then took the patient's hand in his own and stuck a needle into the fleshy part of his thumb. As the blood oozed from the puncture, the schizophrenic gasped and exclaimed, "Well, what do you know! Dead people *do* bleed!"

There may be times when the reader will find himself holding similar "conversations" with his uncomprehending adolescent. These moments usually occur while trying to explain why he must be home by a certain hour—or why he should keep his room straight—or why he can't have the car on Friday night—or why it doesn't *really* matter that he wasn't invited to the smashing party given by the senior sweetheart, Helen Highschool. These issues defy reason, responding instead to the dynamic emotional, social, and chemical forces which propel them.

On the other hand, we can't afford to abandon our communicative efforts just because parents and teens have difficulty understanding one another. We simply must remain "in touch" during these turbulent years. This is especially true for the pleasant and happy child who seemingly degenerates overnight into a sour and critical fourteen-year-old anarchist (a common phenomenon). Not only are parents distressed by this radical change but the child is often worried about it too. He may be confused by the resentment and hostility which has become so much a part of his personality. He clearly needs the patient reassurance of a loving parent who can explain the "normality" of this agitation and help him ventilate the accumulated tension.

But how can this be accomplished? 'Tis a difficult question to answer. The task of prying open the door of communication with an angry adolescent can require more tact and skill than any other assignment in parenthood. The typical reaction by mothers and fathers is to be drawn into endless verbal battles that leave them exhausted but without strategic advantage. There has to be a better way of communicating than shouting at one another. Let me propose an alternative that might be workable in this situation.

For purposes of illustration, suppose that Brian is now fourteen years old and has entered a period of rebelliousness and defiance as described above. He is breaking rules right and left, and seems to hate the entire family. He becomes angry when his parents discipline him, of course, but even during tranquil times he seems to resent them for merely being there. Last Friday night he arrived home an hour beyond his deadline, but refused to explain why he was late or make apologetic noises. What course of action would be best for his parents to take?

Let's assume that you are Brian's father. I would recommend that you invite him out to breakfast on a Saturday morning, leaving the rest of the family at home. It would be best if this event could occur during a relatively tranquil time, certainly not in the midst of a hassle or intergenerational battle. Admit that you have some important matters to discuss with him which can't be communicated adequately at home, but don't "tip your hand" before Saturday morning. Then at the appropriate moment during breakfast, convey the following messages (or an adaptation thereof):

A. Brian, I wanted to talk to you this 'morning because of the changes that are taking place in you and in our home. We both know that the past few weeks have not been very pleasant. You have been angry most of the time and have become disobedient and rude. And your mother and I haven't done so well either. We've become irritable and we've said things that we've regretted later. This is not what God wants of us as parents, or of you as our son. There has to be a more creative way of solving our problems. That's why we're all here.

B. As a place to begin, Brian, I want you to understand what is happening. You have gone into a new period of life known as adolescence. This is the final phase of childhood, and it is often a very stormy and difficult few years. Nearly everyone on earth goes through these rough years during their early teens, and you are right on schedule at this moment. Many of the problems you face today were predictable from the day you were born, simply because growing up has never been an easy thing to do. There are even greater pressures on kids today than when we were young. I've said that to tell you this: we understand you and love you as much as we ever did, even though the past few months have been difficult in our home.

C. What is actually taking place, you see, is that you have had a taste of freedom. You are tired of being a little boy who was told what to wear and when to go to bed and what to eat. That is a healthy attitude which will help you grow up. However, now you want to be your own boss and make your own decisions without interference from anyone. *Brian, you will get what you want in a very short time.* You are fourteen now, and you'll soon be fifteen and seventeen and nineteen. You will be grown in a twinkling of an eye, and we will no longer have any responsibility for you. The day is coming when you will marry whomever you wish, go to whatever school you choose, select the profession or job that suits you. Your mother and I will not try to make those decisions for you. We will respect your adulthood. Furthermore, Brian, the closer you get to those days, the more freedom we plan to give you. You have more privileges now than you had last year, and that trend will continue. We will soon set you free, and you will be accountable only to God and yourself.

D. But, Brian, you must understand this message: *you are not grown yet*. During the past few weeks, you have wanted your mother and me to leave you alone—to let you stay out half the night if you chose—to fail in school—to carry no responsibility at home. And you have "blown up" whenever we have denied even your most extreme demands. The truth of the matter is, you have wanted us to grant you twenty-year-old freedom during the fourteenth year, although you still expect to have your shirts ironed and your meals fixed and your bills paid. You have wanted the best of both worlds with none of the responsibilities. So what are we to do? The easiest thing would be for us to let you have your way. There would be no hassles and no conflict and no more frustration. Many parents of fourteen-year-old sons and daughters have done just that. But we *must not* yield to this temptation. You are not ready for that complete independence, and we would be showing hatred for you (instead of love) if we surrendered at this time. We would regret our mistake for the rest of our lives, and you would soon blame us, too. And as you know, you have two younger sisters who are watching you very closely, and must be protected from the things you are teaching them.

E. Besides, Brian, God has given us a responsibility as parents to do what is right for you, and He is holding us accountable for the way we do that job. I want to read you an important passage from the Bible which describes a father named Eli who did not discipline and correct his two unruly teen-age sons. (Read the dramatic story from the Living Bible, 1 Samuel 2:12–

17, 22–25, 27–34; 3:11–14; 4:1–3 and 10–22.) It is very clear that God was angry at Eli for permitting his sons to be disrespectful and disobedient. Not only did He allow the sons to be killed in battle, but He also punished their father for not accepting his parental responsibilities. This assignment to parents can be found throughout the Bible: mothers and fathers are expected to train their children and discipline them when required. What I'm saying is that God will not hold us blameless if we let you behave in ways that are harmful to yourself and others.

F. That brings us to the question of where we go from this moment. I want to make a pledge to you, here and now: your mother and I intend to be more sensitive to your needs and feelings than we've been in the past. We're not perfect, as you well know, and it is possible that you will feel we have been unfair at one time or another. If that occurs, you can express your views and we will listen to you. We want to keep the door of communication standing wide open between us. When you seek a new privilege, I'm going to ask myself this question, "Is there any way I can grant this request without harming Brian or other people?" If I can permit what you want in good conscience, I will do so. I will compromise and bend as far as my best judgment will let me.

G. But hear this, Brian. There will be a few matters that *cannot* be compromised. There will be occasions when I will have to say "no." And when those times come, you can expect me to stand like the Rock of Gibraltar. No amount of violence and temper tantrums and door slamming will change a thing. In fact, if you choose to fight me in those remaining rules, then I promise that you will lose dramatically. Admittedly you're too big and grown up to spank, but I can still make you uncomfortable. And that will be my goal. Believe me, Brian, I'll lie awake nights figuring how to make you miserable. I have the courage and the determination to do my job during these last few years you are at home, and I intend to use all of my resources for this purpose, if necessary. So it's up to you. We can have a peaceful time of cooperation at home, or we can spend this last part of your childhood in unpleasantness and struggle. Either way, you *will* arrive home when you are told, and you *will* carry your share of responsibility in the family and you *will* continue to respect your mother and me.

H. Finally, Brian, let me emphasize the message I gave you in the beginning. We love you more than you can imagine, and we're going to remain friends during this difficult time. There is so much pain in the world today. Life involves disappointment and loss and rejection and aging and sickness and ultimately death. You haven't felt much of that discomfort yet, but you'll taste it soon enough. So with all that heartache outside our door, let's not bring more of it on ourselves. We need each other. We need you, and believe it or not, you still need us occasionally. And that, I suppose, is what we wanted to convey to you this morning. Let's make it better from now on.

I. Do you have things that need to be said to us?

The content of this message should be modified to fit individual circumstances and the needs of particular adolescents. Furthermore, the responses of children will vary tremendously from person to person. An "open" boy or girl may reveal his deepest feelings at such a moment of communication, permitting a priceless time of catharsis and ventilation. On the other hand, a stubborn, defiant, proud adolescent may sit immobile with head downward. But even if your teen-ager remains stoic or hostile, at least the cards have been laid on the table and parental intentions explained.

We must deal now with the child who listens to these parental messages but then defiantly chooses to fight it out, anyway.

3. Link Behavior with Desirable and Undesirable Consequences

As stated in the preceding section (and in an earlier chapter) one of the most common mistakes of parenthood is to be drawn into verbal battles with our children which leave us exhausted but without strategic advantage. Let me say it again: don't yield to this impulse. Don't argue with your teen. Don't subject him to perpetual threats and finger-wagging accusations and insulting indictments. And most important, don't *nag* him endlessly. Adolescents hate to be nagged by "Mommie" and "Daddy"! When that occurs, they typically "protect" themselves by appearing deaf. Thus, the quickest way to terminate all communication between generations is to follow a young person around the house, repeating the same monotonous messages of disapproval with the regularity of a cuckoo clock.

During the 1950s a popular rock and roll song cleverly expressed this kind of harassment of a teen-ager by his nagging parents. It was entitled, appropriately, "Yakety Yak (Don't Talk Back)" and was recorded initially by the Coasters.[1]

> Take out the papers and the trash
>   or you don't get no spending cash;

If you don't scrub that kitchen floor
   you ain't gonna rock and roll no more.
Yakety Yak (Don't talk back)!

Just finish cleaning up your room
   let's see that dust fly with that broom.
Get all that garbage out of sight
   or you don't go out Friday night.
Yakety Yak (Don't talk back)!

You just put on your coat and hat
   and walk yourself to the laundry mat.
And when you finish doing that
   Bring in the dog and put out the cat.
Yakety Yak (Don't talk back)!

Don't give me no dirty looks;
   Your father's hip, he knows what cooks.
Just tell your hoodlum friends outside
   You ain't got time to take a ride.
Yakety Yak (Don't talk back)! Yakety Yak Yakety Yak

If Yakety-yaking is not the answer, then what is the proper response to slovenliness, disobedience, defiance, and irresponsibility? That question takes us back to the threat, implied to Brian, that his father would make him "miserable" if he did not cooperate. Don't let the news leak out, but the tools available to implement that promise are relatively weak. Since it is unwise (and unproductive) to spank a teen-ager, parents can only manipulate environmental circumstances when discipline is required. They have the keys to the family automobile and can allow their son or daughter to use it (or be chauffered in it). They may grant or withhold privileges, including permission to go to the beach or to the mountains or to a friend's house or to a party. They control the family purse and can choose to share it or loan it or dole it or close it. They can "ground" their adolescent or deny him the use of the telephone or television for awhile.

Now obviously, these are not very influential "motivators," and are at times totally inadequate for the situation at hand. After we have appealed to reason and cooperation and family loyalty, all that remains are relatively weak methods of "punishment." We can only link behavior of our kids with desirable and undesirable consequences and hope the connection will be of sufficient influence to elicit their cooperation.

If that sounds pretty wobbly-legged, let me admit what I am implying: a willful, angry, sixteen-year-old boy or girl *CAN* win a confrontation with his parents today, if worst comes to worst. The law leans ever more in the direction of emancipation of the teen-ager. He can leave home in many areas and avoid being returned. He can drink and smoke pot and break many other civil laws before he is punished by society. His girl friend can obtain birth control pills in many states without her parents' knowledge or permission, and if that fails, she can slip into a clinic for an unannounced abortion. Very few "adult" privileges and vices can be denied a teen-ager who has the passion for independence and a will to fight.

How different was the situation when Billy-Joe was raised on the farm in days of old, living perhaps eight or ten miles by horseback from the home of his nearest contemporary. His dad, Farmer Brown, impressed by his own authority, could "talk sense" to his rebellious boy without the interference of outside pressures. There is no doubt that it was much easier for father and son to come to terms while sitting on a plow at the far end of Forgotten Field.

But today, every spark of adolescent discontent is fanned into a smoldering flame. The grab for the teen dollar has become big business, enticing magazines, record companies, radio, television, and concert entrepreneurs to cater to each youthful whim. And, of course, masses of high school students congregate idly in the city and patronize those obliging companies. They have become a force to be considered. Only last week, 2500 teens "crashed" a party given in my neighborhood, strewing beer cans and broken glass up and down the block. When the Chief of Police was asked why he didn't break up the disturbance, he replied, (to my recollection):

"What were we to do? There were twenty-four policemen against 2500 kids. We made a few arrests, but each student seized had to be escorted to the station by two men. It was just not feasible to control the entire mob. Furthermore, it is not illegal to stand in a crowd of young people. Before taking any action, we had to witness a specific offense being committed there in the dark, and then catch the particular person responsible. The rest of the crowd considered policemen to be enemies, of course, and interfered with the apprehensions. All in all, it was an impossible assignment."

If policemen are unable to control teens today, then parents are in an even more delicate position. Unless their sons and daughters have an inner tug toward cooperation and responsibility, the situation can get bloody very quickly. But where does that voice of restraint originate? It has been my contention that the early years of childhood are vital to the establishment of respect between generations. This book, in effect, is devoted to helping parents of strong-willed children create a relationship of love and control during the preteen years that will contribute toward adolescent sanity. Without that foundation—without a touch of awe in the child's perception of his parent—then the balance of power and control is definitely shifted toward the younger combatant. I would be doing a disservice to my readers if I implied otherwise.

On the other hand, we must do the best job we can during the teen years, even if that foundation has not been laid. Our avowed purpose in that situation is to prevent the emerging adult from making costly errors with lifetime implications, including drug addictions, disastrous early marriage, pregnancy, school failure, alcoholism, etc. There may be occasions when these serious threats require a radical response by mothers and fathers.

My parents were once in that position. When I was sixteen years old, I began to play some "games" which they viewed with alarm. I had not yet crossed the line into all-out rebellion, but I was definitely leaning in that direction. My father was a minister who was traveling consistently during that time, and when my mother informed him of my sudden defiance, he reacted decisively. He cancelled his three-year speaking schedule and accepted a pastoral assignment which permitted him to be home with me for my last two years in high school. He sold our home and moved the family seven hundred miles south to give me a fresh environment, new friends, and the opportunity to hunt and fish. I didn't know that I had motivated this relocation, but now I understand my parents' reasoning and appreciate their caring enough to sacrifice their home, job, friends, and personal desires, just for my welfare. This was one way they revealed their love for me at a critical stage of my development.

The story does not end there, of course. It was difficult making new friends in a strange high school at the beginning of my junior year. I was lonely and felt out of place in a town that failed to acknowledge my arrival. My mother sensed this feeling of friendlessness and in her characteristic way, was "hurting" with me. One day after we had been in the new community for about two weeks, she took my hand and pressed a piece of paper into the palm. She looked in my eyes and said, "This is for you. Don't tell anybody.

Just take it and use it for anything you want. It isn't much, but I want you to get something that looks good to you."

I unfolded the "paper," which turned out to be a twenty-dollar bill. It was money that my mother and father didn't have, considering the cost of the move and the small salary my dad was to be paid. But no matter. I stood at the top of their list of priorities during those stormy days. We all know that money won't buy friends and twenty dollars (even then) did not change my life significantly. Nevertheless, my mother used that method of saying to me, "I feel what you feel; I know it's difficult right now, but I'm your friend and I want to help." Every troubled teen should be so fortunate as to have parents who are still pulling for him and praying for him and feeling for him, even when he has become most unlovable.

In summary, I have been suggesting that parents be willing to take whatever corrective action is required, but to avoid nagging, moaning, groaning, and growling when possible. Anger does not motivate teen-agers! How foolish it is, for example, for the vice principal of Kamakaze High School to stand screaming in the parking lot as students roar past in their cars. He can solve the speeding problem once and for all by placing a bump in the road which will tear the wheels off their love-buggies if they ignore its sinister presence. In Russia, by the way, students who are convicted of taking drugs are placed at the end of a waiting list to obtain cars. This policy has had a remarkable impact on the unpopularity of narcotics there, I'm told. These two illustrations contain the key to adolescent discipline, if in fact one exists. It involves the manipulation of circumstances, whatever they may be, to influence the behavior of youngsters, combined with an appeal to love and reason and cooperation and compromise. It ain't much, as they say, but it's all we've got.

4. Prepare for Adolescence

At the risk of being redundant, I feel I must repeat a word of advice offered in my book *Hide or Seek*. I stressed there the importance of preparing the preteen-ager for adolescence. We know, as parents, that the teen years can be extremely distressing and tense, yet we typically keep that information to ourselves. We fail to brace our children properly for the social pressures and physical changes that await their arrival at puberty. Instead, we send them skipping unsuspectingly into this hazardous terrain, like Little Red Riding Hood dancing merrily down the path with a basket of goodies. If that sweet child's parents had warned her about the Big Bad Wolf, she might have noticed that Grandmummie had grown hairier and produced a tail since they last met. (I've often wondered what that old woman must have looked like, considering she could have been confused with a wolf by a member of her own family.) Instead, naive Little Red practically climbed into Lobo's mouth to examine the size of his (her) fangs and was saved by the woodsman at the last second. In real life, unfortunately, the story does not usually end with a dramatic rescue and a "happy ever after" conclusion.

It should be our purpose to help our kids avoid the adolescent "wolves" which threaten to devour them. Great strides can be made in that direction by taking the preteen-ager away from home for at least one day for the purpose of discussing the experiences and events that are approaching. These conversations are most productive when scheduled immediately prior to puberty and should be planned carefully to expose the major "stress points" of adolescence. To assist with this task, I have prepared a six-cassette tape album entitled "Preparing for Adolescence," which deals with topics to be presented. It is my understanding that this series, published by One Way Library, is one of the best selling tape albums in America today. Why? Simply because the preadolescent is in such a delicate period of life; nevertheless, very few Christian materials have been directed to his specific needs or expressed in language he can comprehend.

The subjects discussed on the six tapes are listed below, which will also provide suggested topics for parents who want to handle the assignment without recorded assistance.

Tape #1   *The Canyon of Inferiority.* This tape discusses the widespread feelings of inferiority among adolescents, and why this low self-esteem occurs. It also suggests how to overcome a lack of confidence. Older teen-agers should hear this tape, as well.

Tape #2   *Conformity in Adolescence.* This second tape reveals the enormous peer pressure experienced during the teen-age years. The dangers of group pressure, including drug abuse and alcoholism, are discussed.

Tape #3   *Explanation of Puberty.* This tape is devoted to an in-depth presentation of the physical changes which often frighten the uninformed child. Fears of abnormality, disease and freakishness (such as very early or late development) are pacified and relieved. Sexual development is also discussed openly and confidently, including an explanation of menstruation, nocturnal emissions, masturbation, size of breasts and reproductive organs, etc. This understanding can prevent years of suffering and unnecessary worry if presented at the proper time.

Tape #4   *The Meaning of Love*. This tape is designed to clarify the ten most common misconceptions about romantic love. Many adults will enjoy this discussion.

Tape #5   *The Search for Identity*. This tape serves as a wrap-up presentation, discussing the other emotions that so frequently accompany adolescence.

Tape #6   *Rap Session*. This final tape is perhaps the most interesting presentation in the album. Four teenagers gathered for a rap session in my home, discussing their early experiences as an adolescent. Their previous fears, embarrassment and anxieties are exposed in an open and lively interaction.

I have not wanted this section to sound like an advertisement for my own creative effort, although I suppose that is what it is. However, I have offered this recommendation simply because the preteen-ager needs more attention than he is getting. The tranquillity of his next six or eight years may depend on the orientation he is given at the gateway to adolescence. Thus, whether my tapes are used or not, an effort should be made by parents, teachers, and churches to pacify the fears and doubts and pressures of the teen experiences. (The "Preparing for Adolescence" album can be obtained at many Christian bookstores, or ordered directly from the address provided on the final page of this book.)

This brings us to the concluding recommendation of *The Strong-willed Child*, which also deals with the concluding responsibility of parenthood.

5. "Hold On" with an Open Hand

The most common mistake made by parents of "older" teen-agers (sixteen to nineteen years of age) is in refusing to grant them the independence and maturity they require. Our inclination as loving guardians is to hold our kids too tightly, despite their attempts to squirm free. We try to make all their decisions and keep them snugly beneath our wings and prevent even the possibility of failure. And in so doing, we force our young adults into one of two destructive patterns: either they passively accept our overprotection and remain dependent "children" into adult life, or else they rise up in great wrath to reject our bondage and interference. They lose on both counts. On the one hand they become emotional cripples who are incapable of independent thought, and on the other they grow into angry and guilt-ridden adults who have severed ties with the families they need. Indeed, parents who refuse to grant appropriate independence to their older adolescents are courting disaster not only for their children, but also for themselves.

Let me state it more strongly: I believe American parents are the world's worst when it comes to letting go of their children. This observation was powerfully illustrated in a popular book entitled *What Really Happened to the Class of '65?* The narrative began in the mid-sixties when *Time* Magazine selected the senior class of Palisades High School in Southern California as the focus for its cover story on "Today's Teen-ager." The editors had clearly chosen the cream of the crop for their report. These graduating young men and women lived in one of the wealthiest school districts in America, with an average income of $42,000 per family in 1965 (which would exceed $100,-000 today). Listed among the members of their class were the children of many famous people, including James

Arness, Henry Miller, Karl Malden, Betty Hutton, Sterling Hayden, and Irving Wallace. These students were part of the most beautiful, healthiest, best educated, and most affluent generation in the history of the world, and they knew it. Little wonder that *Time* perceived them to be standing "on the fringe of a golden era" as they left high school and headed for college. Their future sparkled like the sunrise on a summer day.

But that was in 1965. Now we can ask, what *really* happened to the golden young graduates of that year? Two members of their class, Michael Medved and David Wallechinsky, have sought to answer that precise question. Their book presents a follow-up report on thirty of their fellow graduates, ten years after leaving Palisades High School. The result is a fascinating (although profane and vulgar) commentary on a generation of overindulged kids, not only from Pacific Palisades but from all across the United States. It focuses on the major stereotypes which populate every American secondary school, including the gorgeous cheerleader, the cool quarterback, the Jewish intellectual, the goof-off, the dreamboat, the flirt, the underachiever and the wild girl (who made love to 425 boys before losing count). One by one, their private lives and personal histories are revealed.

The outcome of this investigation is striking. This class of 1965, far from entering a "golden era," has been plagued by personal tragedy and emotional unrest. In fact, the students who graduated from American high schools in that year may be the most unstable and "lost" group of young men and women ever produced in our country. A few weeks after this group received their diplomas, our cities began to burn during the long hot summer of racial strife. That signaled the start of the chaos to come. They entered college at a time when drug abuse was not only prevalent but became almost universal for students and teachers alike. Intellectual deterioration was inevitable in this narcotic climate. The Viet Nam war soon heated campus passions to an incendiary level, generating anger and disdain for the government, the President, the military, both political parties, and indeed, the American way of life. That hostility gave rise to bombings and riotings and burning of "establishment" edifices. This generation of college students had already witnessed the brutal assassination of their romantic idol, John F. Kennedy, when they were barely sixteen years old. Then at a critical point in their season of passion, they lost two more beloved heroes, Robert Kennedy and Martin Luther King. Those murders were followed by the killing of students at Kent State University and the street wars that punctuated the 1968 Democratic Convention. These violent convulsions reached their overt culmination in the wake of President Nixon's military foray into Cambodia, which virtually closed down American campuses.

Accompanying this social upheaval was a sudden disintegration of moral and ethical principles, such as has never occurred in the history of mankind. All at once, there were no definite values. There were no standards. No absolutes. No rules. No traditional beliefs on which to lean. Nor could anyone over thirty even be trusted. And as will be recalled, some bright-eyed theologians chose that moment of confusion to announce the death of God. It was a distressing time to be young—to be groping aimlessly in search of personal identity and a place in the sun.

That's what really happened to the class of '65. And their personal lives reflect the turmoil of the times. In case after case, they have tasted the sordid and seamy offerings of a valueless society. They have been hooked on heroin, LSD, barbiturates, and alcohol. They represent broken marriages and sexual extravaganzas and experimental life styles. They produced unwanted children who hadn't the slightest chance of being raised properly. Eleven percent of the class has served time in jail, and one individual (the school's most popular "dreamboat") committed suicide in 1971. Eighteen members admit to having been hospitalized for psychiatric treatment. Thus, a former teacher at Palisades High School characterized the decade from 1965–1975 as "the saddest years of the century." I certainly agree.

My reason for describing this depressing era in such detail is to help us learn from the mistakes of that period. Unfortunately the conditions that produced it are still evident today! You see, the problem was not only powered by disruptive social forces, but was also caused by parental failure to allow the class of 1965 to grow up. Although the older generation exercised very little influence over their sons and daughters after graduation, they nevertheless failed to emancipate them. An amazingly consistent pattern is evident throughout the book, with Moms and Dads bailing their kids out of jail, paying their bills, making it unnecessary to work, and encouraging them to live at home again. They offered volumes of unsolicited advice to accompany their undeserved and unappreciated material gifts. Consider the following quotations from five individuals which reveal parental overindulgence and interference:

> 1. During the final moments of our conversation, Lisa's mother came into the house carrying a bag of groceries for her (twenty-five-year-old) daughter . . . Despite her hammer blows against convention, (Lisa) had always been dependent on her parents . . . to get her out of jail, to shelter her in times of stress, to support her habits, and nurture her ambitions. For all Lisa's rebellion, she had won little independence. She said, "I will say that my mother has been very helpful financially. My parents understand. Like I told you before: I've never held a job for more than three months. I'm an artist."

2. "Actually I think a lot of my problems had to do with the Palisades. There is no doubt in my mind that if I hadn't grown up in such a protected background, I would have been better off. I would have chosen something like Neil's background. His family is a little more ordinary, a little more middleclass. They have this feeling that at seventeen or eighteen you're grown up. You make your own decisions. With me, I was just a "nice" girl who never got into trouble and was never allowed to make any mistakes. So when I started making decisions for myself . . . I went haywire."

3. "I paid no attention to school. My parents had given me fourteen hundred dollars so I would learn how to take care of money. During the six months I was supposed to be going to school, mostly what I did was . . . spend money. It was the most lovely and free and learningful time of my life. Consequently, I did not achieve too much scholastically. As a matter of fact, all of my teachers gave me F's."

4. "Because I could rely on my parents to give me concrete financial support, I early on developed an aversion to working in a structured situation where I had to be some place at a certain time. I didn't like being asked to sell my life in order to buy back my life from the patriarchs who have turned the economy into a munitions plant."

5. "For six months it was cool [referring to drug abuse]. There was no thievery or crashing cars or falling down stairs. But after that I was really hooked. I finally crashed my parents' Pegueot. A nice car. No one was hurt in the accident. I remember bouncing around inside the car as it rolled over. I also remember finding myself out on the street before the police came and remembering that I had a marijuana joint in my pocket and not wanting to get busted for possession. I threw the joint away and did not get busted, but I could not walk a straight line at the police station. They put me in a tank overnight. My father came down and he was so exasperated and horrified at what I had become that he said through the jail grille that I could just stay there. *This was quite a blow to me, because they had always rescued me in the past.*"

One of the class members, Jamie Kelso, accurately summarized the circumstances that kept his age-mates in a state of perpetual dependency:

> "For two reasons it was certain that many members of the class of '65 would become parasites living off their parents or the tax-payers. First, their parents prevented the children from understanding the problem of survival by always solving their problems for them. By age eighteen, a man or woman's character is largely set. *If, up to this age, the parents have freely provided cars, tuition, allowances, vacations, clothes, apartments, and entertainment, then they shouldn't be too surprised when they discover that their son or daughter is a moral cripple.* The second reason to expect parasites is the unreality of what was taught at Pali. Bearing with us from high school no philosophical substance, and irrationality as method, we were easy prey for the sharpies in the university, and sitting ducks for the spiritual con men of our time."[2]

Jamie Kelso is a very perceptive young man. He has observed the necessity for parents to set their children free—to allow them to make mistakes and to learn from their failures even when they are very young. This experience is vital because, in a sense, all of childhood is a preparation for adolescence and beyond. Thus, parents would be wise to remember that the day is fast approaching when the child they have raised will pack his suitcase and leave home, never to return. And as he walks through the door to confront the outside world, he will no longer be accountable to parental authority and supervision. He can do what he chooses. No one can require him to eat properly, or get his needed rest, or find a job, or live responsibly, or serve God. He will sink or swim on his own. This sudden independence can be devastating for some individuals who have not been properly prepared for it. But how can a mother and father train an individual so that he won't go wild in the first dizzying months of freedom? How can they equip him for that moment of emancipation?

The best time to begin preparing a child for the ultimate release is during toddlerhood, before a relationship of dependence is established. However, the natural inclination of parents is to do the opposite. As Renshaw wrote,

> It may be easier for the child to feed himself; more untidy for him to dress himself; less clean when he attempts to bathe himself; less perfect for him to comb his hair; but unless his mother learns to sit on her hands and allow the child to cry and to try, she will overdo for the child, and independence will be delayed.[3]

This process of granting appropriate independence must continue through the elementary school years. Parents should permit their kids to go to summer camp even though it might be "safer" to keep them at home. Likewise, boys and girls ought to be allowed to spend the night with their friends when invited. They should make their own beds, take care of their animals, and do their homework. In short, the parental purpose should be to grant increasing freedom and responsibility year by year, so that when the child gets beyond adult control, he will no longer need it.

When this assignment is handled properly, a high school senior should be virtually emancipated, even though he still lives with his parents. This was the case during my last year at home. When I was seventeen years of age, my parents tested my independence by going on a two-week trip, and leaving me behind. They loaned me the family car, and gave me permission to invite my (male) friends to spend the fourteen nights at our home. I remember being surprised by this move and the obvious risks they were taking. I could have thrown fourteen wild parties and wrecked the car and destroyed our residence. Frankly, I wondered if they were wise to give me that much latitude. I did behave responsibly (although our house suffered the effects of some typical adolescent horseplay).

After I was grown and married, I asked my mother why she took those risks—why she left me unsupervised for two weeks. She smiled and replied, "Because I knew in approximately one year you would be leaving for college, where you would have complete freedom with no one to tell you how to behave. And I wanted to expose you to that independence while you were still under my influence." Her intuitive wisdom was apparent, once more. She was preparing me for the ultimate release, which often causes an overprotected young man or woman to behave foolishly the moment they escape the heavy hand of authority.

Our objective as parents, then, is to do *nothing* for boys and girls which they can profit from doing for themselves. I admit the difficulty of implementing this policy. Our deep love for our children makes us tremendously vulnerable to their needs. Life inevitably brings pain and sorrow to little people, and we hurt when they hurt. When others ridicule them or laugh at them, when they feel lonely and rejected, when they fail at something important, when they cry in the midnight hours, when physical harm threatens their existence—these are the trials which seem unbearable to those of us who watch from the sidelines. We want to rise like a mighty shield to protect them from life's sting— to hold them snugly within the safety of our embrace. Yet there are times when we must let them struggle. Children can't grow without taking risks. Toddlers can't walk initially without falling down. Students can't learn without facing some hardships. And ultimately, an adolescent can't enter young adulthood until we release him from our protective custody. But as I have indicated, parents in the Western world find it difficult to let their offspring face and conquer the routine challenges of everyday living. As Jamie Kelso said of the class of 1965, "Their parents prevented the children from understanding the problem of survival by always solving their problems for them." They also failed to provide a moral and spiritual foundation—a reason for living—which Jamie referred to as having "no philosophical substance."

Let me offer three phrases which will guide our parenting efforts during the final era of childhood. The first is simply, "Hold on with an open hand." This implies that we still care about the outcome during early adulthood, but we must not clutch our children too tightly. Our grip must be relaxed. We should pray for them, love them, and even offer advice to them when it is sought. But the responsibility to make personal decisions must be borne by the next generation and they must also accept the consequences of those choices.

Another phrase expressing a similar concept is, "Hold them close and let them go." This seven-word suggestion could almost represent the theme of my book. Parents should be deeply involved in the lives of their young children, providing love and protection and authority. But when those children reach their late teens and early twenties, the cage door must be opened to the world outside. That is the most frightening time of parenthood, particularly for Christian mothers and fathers who care so deeply about the spiritual welfare of their families. How difficult it is to await an answer to the question, "Did I train them properly?" The tendency is to retain control in order to avoid hearing the wrong reply to that all-important question. Nevertheless, our sons and daughters are more likely to make proper choices when they do not have to rebel against our meddling interference.

The third phrase could easily have been one of King Solomon's Proverbs, although it does not appear in the Bible. It states, "If you love something, set it free. If it comes back to you, then it's yours. If it doesn't return, then it never was yours in the first place." This little statement contains great wisdom. It reminds me of a day last year when a wild coyote pup trotted in front of my house. He had strayed into our residential area from the nearby mountains. I managed to chase him into our backyard where I trapped him in a corner. After fifteen or twenty minutes of effort, I succeeded in placing a collar and leash around his neck. He fought the noose with all his strength, jumping, diving, gnawing, and straining at the tether. Finally, in exhaustion, he submitted to his servitude. He was my captive, to the delight of the neighborhood children. I kept the little rascal for an entire day and considered trying to make a pet of him. However, I contacted an authority on coyotes, who told me the chances were very slim that I could tame his wild streak. Obviously, I could have kept him chained or caged, but he would never really have belonged to me. Thus, I asked a game warden to return the lop-eared creature to his native territory in the canyons above Los Angeles. You see, his "friendship" meant nothing to me unless I could set him free and retain him by his own choice.

My point is that love demands freedom. It is true not only of relationships between animals and man, but also in all human interactions. For example, the quickest way to destroy a romantic love between a husband and wife is for one partner to clamp a steel cage around the other. I've seen hundreds of women trying unsuccessfully to demand love and fidelity from their husbands. It won't work. Think back to your dating experiences before marriage. Do you recall that any romantic relationship was doomed the moment one partner began to worry about losing the other, phoning six or eight times a day and hiding behind trees to see who was competing for the lover's attention? That hand wringing performance will devastate a perfectly good love affair in a matter of days. To repeat, *love demands freedom.*

Why else did God give us the choice of either serving Him or rejecting His companionship? Why did He give Adam and Eve the option of eating forbidden fruit in the Garden of Eden, instead of forcing their obedience? Why didn't He just make men and women His slaves who were programmed to worship at His feet? The answers are found in the meaning of love. God gave us a free choice because there is no significance to love that knows no alternative. It is only when we come to Him because we hungrily seek His fellowship and communion that the relationship has any validity. Isn't this the meaning of Proverbs 8:17, whereby He says, "I love them that love me; and those that seek me early shall find me?" That is the love that only freedom can produce. It cannot be demanded or coerced or required or programmed against our will. It can only be the product of a free choice which is honored even by the Almighty.

The application of this perspective to older adolescents (especially those in their early twenties) should be obvious. There comes a point where our record as parents is in the books, our training has been completed, and the moment of release has arrived. As I did with the young coyote, we must unsnap the leash and remove the collar. If our "child" runs, he runs. If he marries the wrong person, he marries the wrong person. If he takes drugs, he takes drugs. If he goes to the wrong school, or rejects his faith, or refuses to work, or squanders his inheritance on liquor and prostitutes, then he must be permitted to make these destructive choices. *But it is not our task to pay the bills, ameliorate the consequences, or support his folly.*

A lesson can be learned from the prodigal son of whom Jesus spoke. He became so desperately hungry when he ran out of money that even the pigs' food began to look good to him. Nevertheless, "no one gave him anything." There were no food stamps or welfare checks or unemployment programs to support his life as a swinger, and he was systematically starving. It was in that state of utter need that "he came to his senses." Deprivation has a way of bringing us back to the basics, or in the case of the prodigal son, back to Daddy. We parents would be wise to follow the example of the loving father in this story, who symbolizes God Himself. First, he set the boy free with no strings attached. Second, he allowed him to suffer the consequences of his own foolishness even though he could, as a wealthy farmer, have sent his servants to bail him out. And third, he revealed his immeasurable love by welcoming home his repentant son without insults or accusations, saying joyfully, "He was lost and is found!"

In summary, let me say that adolescence is not an easy time of life for either generation; in fact, it can be downright terrifying. But the key to surviving this emotional experience is to lay the proper foundation and then face it with courage. Even the inevitable rebellion of the teen years can be a healthy factor. This conflict contributes to the process by which an individual changes from a dependent child to a mature adult, taking his place as a co-equal with his parents. Without that friction, the relationship could continue to be an unhealthy "mommie-daddy-child" triad, late into adult life, with serious implications for future marital harmony. If the strain between generations were not part of the divine plan of human development, it would not be so universally prevalent, even in homes where love and authority have been maintained in proper balance.

QUESTIONS

Question: I have a fourteen-year-old daughter, Margretta, who wants to date a seventeen-year-old boy. I don't feel good about letting her go, but I'm not sure just how to respond. What should we say to her?

Answer: Rather than stamping your foot and screaming "No! And that's semi-final!" I would suggest that you sit down with your daughter and work out a reasonable plan for the years ahead and a rationale to support it. You might say, "Margretta, you are fourteen years old and I understand your new interest in boys. That's the way it's supposed to be. However, you are not ready to handle the pressures that an older boy can put on a girl your age." (Explain what you mean if she asks.)

"Your dad and I want to help you get ready for dating in the future, but there are some in-between steps you need to take. You have to learn how to be 'friends' with boys before you become a 'lover' with one. To do this, you should get acquainted in groups of boys or girls your age. We'll invite them to our house or you can go to the homes of others. Then when you are between fifteen and sixteen, you can begin double-dating to places that are chaperoned by adults. And finally, you can go on single dates sometime during your sixteenth year.

"Your dad and I want you to date and have fun with boys, and we intend to be reasonable about this. But you're not ready to plunge into single dating with a high school senior, and we'll just have to find other ways to satisfy your social needs."

Question: We have been concerned by the lack of discipline evident at the junior high and high school level today. What suggestion do you have to reinstate reasonable authority in public education?

Answer: I intend to write another book soon dealing with practical methods of school discipline (which explains the absence of that topic in *The Strong-willed Child*). I will only say here that black activist Jesse Jackson makes more sense than anyone writing on this subject, particularly with reference to discipline in inner-city, "ghetto" schools. Quoted below is a sampling of Rev. Jackson's views as reported by Donald Cole in a recent *Moody Monthly* editorial:

> "Violence and vandalism in the nation's public schools are approaching epidemic proportions," said an article in *U.S. News and World Report* early this year. "And nobody," it added, "knows what to do about it."
>
> Nobody? Not quite. These days Chicago based black activist Jesse Jackson is talking about decadence in the schools, and what he says makes sense, perhaps because it is also biblical.
>
> What is he saying? In a recent speech he recounted his visit to a Los Angeles high school. There he saw students "walking down the halls with their eyes red from marijuana, minds empty and foggy. No self-respect, no bounds. And the debate," he went on, "was not whether they should smoke it, but where!"
>
> When the principal told him how wonderful the students were, Jackson cut her off. "I told her they were little gangsters," he recalls; "that her students weren't wonderful, but that they could be. We've got to change them. Our challenge is to make flowers bloom in the desert!"
>
> Jackson is calling for fundamental changes in people. It's a tall order. He believes that 7 to 9 P.M. or 8 to 10 P.M. should be mandatory citywide study hours "with no radio and TV to interfere." Parents should be required to call at the school for their children's report cards, and if they refuse, committees of parents should visit them to find out why, and, of course, apply a little pressure.
>
> He would ban outlandish clothing: no superfly suits, no platform shoes. "I'm convinced," he says, "that if we begin to instill discipline and responsibility and self-respect, there will be better conduct." Then the learning can begin, and learning is what school is all about.

Jackson scoffs at those who complain that achievement tests are rigged against blacks. "We can't read or write," he says, "because of one of two reasons. Either we are retarded or we don't practice. We do well what we do most—dance, talk, jive, be deceptive. We're not so inferior that we can't learn to read and write, but we're not so superior that we can do it without practicing."

What he wants is new values. "Maybe we should begin to define men by their ability to heal," he declares, "not their ability to kill. Maybe we will say that a man is not a man if he can make a baby; that he is a man if he can provide for a baby, take care of a baby, love the mother."

The heart of his program is parental responsibility. "Care and discipline and chastisement do not cost money," he adds, "they cost new priorities." And that, of course, is just the problem.

If parents in every community were willing to pay the price, a little order could be imposed upon the chaotic schools. But in many families it is the parents who are spiritually bankrupt.

For parents who have some notion of decency and purpose, however, now is the time to respond and seek to exert a holy influence on the local school boards. Those who are Christians should let their lights shine, insisting before school boards and others on a return to first principles. Let the salt of the earth penetrate the public schools; let its tang check the violence and end the vandalism in our schools. Otherwise the system is doomed and all the fine speeches in the world will never save it.[4]

Question: You recommended in *Dare to Discipline* that pre-adolescents be taught the fundamentals of reproduction by watching the birth process in a cat or hamster. Your intentions were honorable, but this suggestion could result in the proliferation of unwanted animals and their starvation and cruel abuse. Those strays that survive in the streets are killed in pounds and vets' offices. I feel you should reconsider this unfortunate position.

Answer: To my complete surprise, that seemingly innocuous recommendation in *Dare to Discipline* has drawn more flak and criticism than all other aspects of the book combined. One dedicated crusader from Denver (she'll know who I mean) selected me as her "project" for the year and badgered me regularly to delete that section of my book. When I resisted, she gave my name to a veterinarian who adopted the cause. Finally, I wrote the woman a letter containing this statement: "Dear Mrs. _____, You win! I surrender! I'll change my recommendation in future publications; you are a credit to bulldogs the world over, and I congratulate you for your tenacity." (I am fulfilling my pledge to her, now.)

Actually, I capitulated because this lady and the others who have written me are absolutely right. There are millions of animals (notably dogs and cats) who roam the streets —hungry, disease-ridden and miserable. Many others will be destroyed in pounds and veterinarians' offices. I don't want to contribute to that unnecessary suffering, and hereby caution parents not to permit animal births unless they intend to care for the little creatures they have produced.

There, Mrs. X, my conscience is clean. Best wishes on your new project.

Question: You mentioned the fact that girls can obtain abortions without parental knowledge or consent in many states. This method of terminating a pregnancy is obviously very controversial now, and I would like to have your *opinion* on the moral issues involved.

Answer: My viewpoint on this extremely important matter has been in a state of evolution during the past ten years. When the controversy initially surfaced, I deliberately withheld judgment until I could consider the issue objectively from every vantage point. I have now completed that examination and find myself absolutely and unequivocably opposed to "abortion on demand," that is, abortion for reasons other than rape, incest, or factors relating to health of the mother and child.

There were many considerations which led to this position, including the impact of abortions on our perception of human life. It is interesting to note, for example, that a woman who plans to terminate her pregnancy usually refers to the life within her as "the fetus." But if she intends to deliver and love and care for the little child, she affectionately calls him "my baby." The need for this distinction is obvious: If we are going to kill a human being without experiencing guilt, we must first strip it of worth and dignity. We must give it a clinical name that denies its personhood. That has been so effectively accomplished in our society that an unborn child during his first six months in gestation can now be sacrificed with no sense of loss on anyone's part. There would be a far greater public outcry if we were destroying puppies or kittens than there is for the million abortions that occur in America each year. Psychiatrist Thomas Szasz reflects the casualness with which we have accepted these deaths by writing, "[abortions] should be available in the same way as, say, an operation for beautification of the nose."[5]

I agree with Francis Schaeffer that the changing legal attitudes toward abortions carry major implications for human life at all levels. If the rights of the unborn child can be sacrificed by reinterpretation by the Supreme Court, why could not other unnecessary people be legislated out of existence? For example, the expense and inconvenience of caring for the severely retarded could easily lead to the same social justification that has encouraged us to kill the unborn (i.e., they will be an expensive nuisance if permitted to live). And how about getting rid of the very old members of our population who contribute nothing to society? And why should we allow deformed infants to live, etc? Perhaps the reader feels those chilling possibilities would never materialize, but I'm not so sure. We already live in a society where some parents will kill an unborn child if they determine through aminiocentesis that its sex is not the one they desired.

There are many other aspects of the abortion issue that underscore its inherent evil, but the most important evidence for me came from the Scripture. Of course the Bible does not address itself directly to the practice of abortions. However, I was amazed to observe how many references are made in both the Old and New Testaments to God's personal acquaintance with children *prior* to birth. Not only was He aware of their gestations but He was specifically knowledgeable of them as unique individuals and personalities.

Consider the following examples:

1. The angel Gabriel said of John the Baptist, "and he shall be filled with the Holy Ghost *even from his mother's womb*" Luke 1:15.

2. The prophet Jeremiah wrote about himself, "The Lord said to me, 'I knew you *before* you were formed within your mother's womb; *before you were born* I sanctified you and appointed you as my spokesman to the world' " Jeremiah 1:4, 5 TLB.

These two individuals were hardly inhuman embryos before their birth. They were already known to the Creator, who had assigned them a life's work by divine decree.

3. In the book of Genesis we are told that Isaac "pleaded with Jehovah to give Rebekah a child, for even after many years of marriage she had no children. Then at last she became pregnant. And it seemed as though children were fighting each other inside her.

   " 'I can't endure this,' she exclaimed. So she asked the Lord about it.

"And he told her, 'The sons in your womb shall become two rival nations. One will be stronger than
the other; and the older shall be the servant of the
younger!' " (Genesis 25:21–23) TLB.

Again, God was aware of the developing personalities in
these unborn twins and foretold their future conflicts. The
mutual hatred of their descendants is still evident in the
Middle East today.

4. Jesus Himself was *conceived* by the Holy Spirit, which
fixes God's involvement with Christ from the time
He was a single cell inside Mary's uterus (Matthew
1:18).

The most dramatic example, however, is found in the 139th
Psalm. King David describes his own prenatal relationship
with God, which is stunning in its impact.

You made all the delicate, inner parts of my body,
and knit them together in my mother's womb. Thank
you for making me so wonderfully complex! It is
amazing to think about. Your workmanship is marvelous—and how well I know it. You were there while
I was being formed in utter seclusion! You saw me
before I was born and scheduled each day of my life
before I began to breathe. Every day was recorded in
your book! (Psalm 139:13–16) TLB

That passage is thrilling to me, because it implies that God
not only scheduled each day of David's life, but He did the
same for *me*. He was there when *I* was being formed in
utter seclusion, and He personally made all the delicate
inner parts of *my* body. Imagine that! The Great Creator
of the universe lovingly supervised my development during
those preconscious days *in utero*, as He did for every human
being on earth. Surely, anyone who can grasp that concept

without sensing an exhilaration is stone-cold dead!

From my point of view, these scriptural references absolutely refute the notion that unborn children do not have a soul or personhood until they are born at full term. I can't believe it! No rationalization can justify detaching a healthy little human being from his place of safety and leaving him to suffocate on a porcelain table. No social or financial considerations can counter-balance our collective guilt for destroying those lives which were being fashioned in the image of God Himself. Throughout the Gospels, Jesus revealed a tenderness toward boys and girls ("suffer little children to come unto me"), and some of his most frightening warnings were addressed to those who would hurt them. It is my deepest conviction that He will not hold us blameless for our wanton infanticide. As He said to Cain, who had killed Abel, "Your brother's blood calls to me from the ground!"

Surely, other Christians have drawn the same conclusion. I must ask, where are those moral leaders who agree with me? Why have pastors and ministers been so timid and mute on this vital matter? It is time that the Christian church found its tongue and spoke in defense of the unborn children who are unable to plead for their own lives.

# 9 The Eternal Source

When a child was born during the 1800s or before, his inexperienced mother was assisted by many friends and relatives who hovered around to offer their advice and support. Very few of these aunts and grandmothers and neighbors had ever read a book on child-rearing, but that was no handicap. They possessed a certain folk wisdom which gave them confidence in handling babies and children. They had a prescribed answer for every situation, whether it proved to be right or wrong. Thus, a young woman was systematically taught how to "mother" by older women who had many years' experience in caring for little people.

With the disappearance of this "extended family," however, the job of motherhood became more frightening. Many young couples today do not have access to such supportive relatives and friends. They live in a mobile society wherein the next-door neighbors are often total strangers. Furthermore, their own mothers and fathers may live in far-away Detroit or Dallas or Portland (and might not be trusted even if they were available to help). Consequently, young parents often experience great anxieties over their lack of preparation for raising children. Dr. Benjamin Spock described their fears in this way: "I can remember mothers who cried on the morning they were to take their baby home. 'I won't know what to do,' they wailed."

This anxiety has brought parents rushing to the "experts" for information and advice. They have turned to pediatricians, psychologists, psychiatrists and educators for answers to their questions about the complexities of parenthood. Therefore, increasing numbers of American children have been reared according to this professional consultation during the past forty years. In fact, no country on earth has embraced the teachings of child psychology and the offerings of family specialists more than has the United States.

It is now appropriate that we ask, "What has been the effect of this professional influence?" One would expect that the mental health of our children would exceed that of individuals raised in nations not having this technical assistance. Such has not been the case. Juvenile delinquency, drug abuse, alcoholism, unwanted pregnancies, mental illness, and suicide are rampant among the young, and continue their steady rise. In many ways, we have made a mess of parenthood! Of course, I would not be so naive as to blame all these woes on the bad advice of the "experts," but I believe they have played a role in creating the problem. Why? *Because in general, behavioral scientists have lacked confidence in the Judeo-Christian ethic and have disregarded the wisdom of this priceless tradition!*

It appears to me that the twentieth century has spawned a generation of professionals who felt qualified to ignore the parental attitudes and practices of more than 2000 years, substituting instead their own wobbly-legged insights of the moment. Each authority, writing from his own limited experience and reflecting his own unique biases, has sold us his guesses and suppositions as though they represented Truth itself. One anthropologist, for example, wrote an incredibly gallish article in *The Saturday Evening Post,* November 1968, entitled "We Scientists Have a Right to Play God." Dr. Edmund Leach stated,

> There can be no source for these moral judgments except the scientist himself. In traditional religion, morality was held to derive from God, but God was only credited with the authority to establish and enforce moral rules because He was also credited with supernatural powers of creation and destruction. Those powers have now been usurped by man, and he must take on the moral responsibility that goes with them.[1]

That paragraph summarizes the many ills of our day. Arrogant men like Edmund Leach have argued God out of existence and put themselves in His exalted place. Armed with that authority, they have issued their ridiculous opinions to the public with unflinching confidence. In turn, desperate families grabbed their porous recommendations like life preservers, which often sank to the bottom, taking their passengers down with them.

These false teachings have included the notions that loving discipline is damaging, and irresponsibility is healthy, and religious instruction is hazardous, and defiance is a valuable ventilator of anger, and all authority is dangerous, and on and on it goes. In more recent years, this humanistic perspective has become even more extreme and anti-Christian. For example, one mother told me recently that she works in a youth project which has obtained the consultative services of a certain psychologist. He has been teaching the parents of kids in the program that in order for young girls to grow up with more healthy attitudes toward sexuality, their fathers should have intercourse with them when they are twelve years of age. If you gasped at that suggestion, be assured that it shocked me also. Yet this is where moral relativism leads—this is the ultimate product of a human endeavor which accepts no standards, honors no cultural values, acknowledges no absolutes, and serves no "god" except the human mind. King David wrote about such foolish efforts in Psalm 14:12: "There is a way that *seemeth* right unto a man, but the end thereof are the ways of death."

Now admittedly, the book you have been reading about the strong-willed child also contains many suggestions and perspectives which I have not attempted to validate or prove. How do my writings differ from the unsupported recommendations of those whom I have criticized? The distinction lies in the *source* of the views being presented. The underlying principles expressed herein are not my own innovative insights which would be forgotten in a brief season or two. Instead, they originated with the inspired biblical writers who gave us the foundation for all relationships in the home. As such, these principles have been handed down generation after generation to this very day. Our ancestors taught it to their children who taught it to their children, keeping the knowledge alive for posterity. Now, unfortunately, that understanding is being vigorously challenged in some circles and altogether forgotten in others.

If I have had a primary mission in writing this book, therefore, it has not been to earn royalty or propagate the name of James Dobson or demonstrate my professional skills. My purpose has been nothing more ambitious than to verbalize the Judeo-Christian tradition regarding discipline of children and to apply those concepts to today's families. This approach has been deeply engrained in the Western culture but has never been expressly written, to my knowledge. It involves control with love, and a reasonable introduction to self-discipline and responsibility, and parental *leadership* which seeks the best interest of the child, and respect for the dignity and worth of every member of the family, and realistic boundaries that are enforced with confident firmness, and finally, a judicious use of rewards and punishment when required for training. It is a system that has existed for more than twenty centuries of parenthood. I did not invent it, nor can I change it. My task has been merely to report what I believe to be the prescription of the Creator Himself. And I am convinced that this understanding will remain viable for as long as mothers and fathers and children cohabit the face of the earth. It will certainly outlive humanism and the puny efforts of mankind to find an alternative.

A Final Comment

We began this discussion 224 pages ago with the story of my dog, Siggie, and his earlier revolutionary tendencies. Perhaps it would be appropriate to close the book with a look at the aging Sigmund today. He is now twelve years old and no longer has the fire of youthful exuberance. In fact, he has developed a progressive "heart leak" and will probably not live more than one more year. So he takes life easy these days, yawning and stretching and going back to sleep in the sun. (We have nicknamed him "Hal" because of his constant halitosis in these declining years.)

It is difficult to explain how a worthless old hound could be so loved by his family, but we're all going to miss little Siggie. (Dog lovers will understand our sentiment, but others will think it foolish.) He is a year older than our eldest child and has been her pal throughout childhood. So we have begun to prepare both children for his inevitable demise.

One day last month the moment of crisis came without warning. I was brushing my teeth in the early morning when I heard Siggie's sharp cry. He can scream like a baby, and my wife rushed to his assistance.

"Jim, come quickly!" she said. "Siggie is having a heart attack!"

I joined her in the family room with toothbrush still in my hand. Siggie was lying just outside his bed and he appeared to be in great pain. He was hunched down on his paws and his eyes were unfocused and glassy. I bent down and petted him gently and agreed that he was probably experiencing heart failure. I was not sure what to do for a dog in the midst of a coronary thrombosis, since the local paramedics are rather sensitive about offering their services to animals. I picked him up and laid him carefully on his bed, and he rolled on one side and remained completely motionless. His feet were held rigidly together, and it did, indeed, look as though the end had come.

I returned to my study to telephone the veterinarian, but Shirley again called me. She had taken a closer look at the immobile dog and discovered the nature of his problem. (Are you ready for this?) There are little claws or toenails on the sides of a dog's legs, and Siggie had somehow managed to get them hooked! That is why he couldn't move, and why he experienced pain when he tried to walk. There is not another dog anywhere in the world who could handcuff (pawcuff?) himself, but with Siggie, anything can happen. Shirley unhooked his toenails and the senile dog celebrated his release by acting like a puppy again.

When I am an old man and I think back on the joys of parenthood—the Christmas seasons and the camping trips and the high-pitched voices of two bubbly children in our home—I will remember a stubborn little dachshund named Sigmund Freud who played such an important role throughout those happy days.

Other Materials for the Family by Dr. James Dobson

Books:

Dare to Discipline, Tyndale House Publishers, 1970. (Over one million copies of this text have been sold.)

Hide or Seek, Self-Esteem for the Child, Fleming H. Revell Publishing Company, 1974.

The Mentally Retarded Child and His Family, Brunner-Mazel Publishers, 1970. (This book was co-edited with Dr. Richard Koch.)

What Wives Wish Their Husbands Knew About Women, Tyndale House Publishers, 1975.

Cassette Tape Recordings:

Dare to Discipline, Vision House Publishers (One Way Library). This album contains six cassette tapes, based on the concepts discussed in the book by the same name.

Preparing for Adolescence, Vision House Publishers (One Way Library). This album contains six cassette tapes, designed to help the preteen-ager prepare for the experience to come.

Self-Esteem for the Child, Vision House Publishers (One Way Library). This album contains four cassette tapes, and presents the ways parents and teachers can maximize self-confidence in children.

What Wives Wish Their Husbands Knew About Women, Vision House Publishers, (One Way Library). This album deals with the basic content of the book by the same name although it contains speeches, radio interviews, and counseling conversations. Dr. Dobson has called this album, "The most important work of my professional life."

These items are available in local bookstores, or can be ordered by writing Box 952, Temple City, California 91780. Dr. Dobson can also be contacted through that address, although he regrets that he is unable to respond to requests for personal consultation.

Notes

CHAPTER 1

1. Raymond Corsini and Genevieve Painter, *Family Circle,* April 1975, p. 26.
2. Dr. Herbert Birch, Dr. Stella Chess, and Dr. Alexander Thomas, *Parent and Child* (New York: Redbook Publishing Company, 1976), "The Individuality Factor," pp. 4, 5, 97).

CHAPTER 2

1. John Valusek, *Parade Magazine,* February 6, 1977, n.p.
2. Dr. James C. Dobson, *Hide or Seek* (Old Tappan, N.J.: Fleming H. Revell Company, 1974), n.p. Used by permission.
3. T. Berry Brazelton, *Toddlers and Parents: A Declaration of Independence* (New York: Delacorte Press, 1974), pp. 101–110.
4. From the *APA Monitor* (published by the American Psychological Association, Washington, D.C.), Vol. 7, No. 4, 1976, n.p.
5. Dr. Luther Woodward, in *Your Child from 2 to 5,* Morton Edwards, editor (New York: Permabooks, 1955), pp. 95, 96.
6. Dr. James Dobson, *Dare to Discipline* (Wheaton, Ill.: Tyndale House Publishers, 1970), p. 20.
7. Reprinted by permission of United Press International.

CHAPTER 3

1. Marguerite and Willard Beecher, *Parents on the Run: A Commonsense Book for Today's Parents* (New York: Crown Publishers, Inc., © 1955 by Marguerite and Willard Beecher), pp. 6–8. Used by permission of Crown Publishers, Inc.
2. Philip Yancey, "Benedict Arnold Seagull," *Campus Life,* © 1975 Youth for Christ International, Wheaton, Illinois. Reprinted by permission.
3. Dr. Milton I. Levine, in *Your Child from 2 to 5,* Morton Edwards, editor, pp. 182–184.

CHAPTER 4

1. Dr. Benjamin Spock, "How Not to Bring up a Bratty Child," *Redbook,* February 1974, pp. 29–31.
2. *Ibid.*
3. *Ibid.*
4. Dobson, *Dare to Discipline,* pp. 37–40.

5. Fitzhugh Dodson, *How to Father* (New York: Nash Publishing Corp., 1974), p. 59. Reprinted by permission.
6. Pat Fabrizio, *Children—Fun or Frenzy?* (Palo Alto, Calif., published by author, 1969).

CHAPTER 5

1. Beecher, n.p.

CHAPTER 6

1. Domeena C. Renshaw, M.D., *The Hyperactive Child* (Chicago: Nelson-Hall Publishers, 1974), pp. 80, 81. Reprinted by permission.
2. *Ibid.*, pp. 118–120.

CHAPTER 7

1. Jim Stingley, "Advocating Children's Liberation," *Los Angeles Times,* July 28, 1974.
2. *Ibid.*
3. Dr. Thomas Gordon, *Parent Effectiveness Training* (New York: David McKay Company, Inc., 1970), pp. 164, 188, 191.
4. *Ibid.*, p. 179.
5. *Ibid.*, n.p.
6. Dr. James Dobson, *Moody Monthly,* reprinted by permission from the October 1976 issue. Copyright 1976, Moody Bible Institute of Chicago.
7. Gordon, pp. 190, 191, 188, 169.
8. Quoted from *Family under Fire,* a conference book by Dr. James Dobson. Other participants quoted were Rev. James Dobson, father of the author, and Dr. Paul Cunningham, pastor, both of whom have given permission for these quotations.

CHAPTER 8

1. "Yakety Yak (Don't Talk Back)," by Jerry Leiber and Mike Stoller. Copyright © 1958 by Tiger Music, Inc. All rights controlled by Unichappell Music, Inc., Quintet Music, Inc., and Freddy Bienstock. International copyright secured. All rights reserved. Used by permission.
2. Michael Medved and David Wallechinsky, *What Really Happened to the Class of '65?* (New York: Random House, Inc., 1976). Quotations used are taken from pp. 30, 55, 155, 160, 283.
3. Renshaw, p. 63.
4. This editorial by C. Donald Cole is reprinted by permission from the September 1976 issue of *Moody Monthly.* Copyright 1976, Moody Bible Institute of Chicago.
5. *Time,* August 22, 1977, p. 49.

CHAPTER 9

1. Dr. Edmund Leach, "We Scientists Have a Right to Play God," *Saturday Evening Post,* November 1968. © 1968 The Curtis Publishing Company, Indianapolis, Ind.